Miracles of Kingman State Prison

Chaplain Paul D. Vescio

Miracles of Kingman State Prison, Preface

Hebrews 11:1 reads, Now Faith is the substance of things hoped for, the evidence of things not seen.

We do not see Abba Father, The Holy Spirit or Christ Yeshua in the flesh, but we see the evidence of their handy work all around us each day. Abba Father placed on my heart to write this story of the incredible things that I personally witnessed while I was an inmate at Kingman State Prison in Kingman Arizona. The greatest miracle of all was the countless number of inmates who gave their lives to Christ while I was there.

As I sit here putting the finishing touches on this book, I realize it's not about myself, fame or fortune, and the stories contained within the pages of this book are not meant to be received as being boastful or bragging by myself in any way. The true purpose of this book is to share with others the evidence of things not seen and in so doing this book will have become a powerful witnessing tool in leading many people to Christ our Lord for the glory God.

Abba Father thank You for all of Your blessings and love in helping me to become the Community Chaplain of God that I am today. Thank You for all of Your guidance, wisdom, and love in helping me to write and publish this incredible story. A story that will one day help in leading many lost souls around the world to the light of Christ Yeshua our Lord. I give all the Praise, Glory, and Honor to You Abba Father... Love Paul, in Christ Yeshua's Holy Name I pray...Amen

It is therefore, my solemn prayer that this book of hope touches the lives of many people in the years to come...Amen   John 14:27

ps There may indeed be some punctuation and grammar errors in my books, but please try to remember no one is perfect including me. Also, I had to change some of the names in this book because I could not reach everyone to ask for their permission in using their real names.

The Miracles of Kingman State Prison Contents

33 Christian Seeds For The Soul was added to
this book.

Nahum 1:7 The LORD is good; a stronghold in
the day of trouble, He cares for those who trust in
Him

The Miracles of Kingman State Prison

& 33 Christian Seeds for the Soul by Chaplain Paul D. Vescio Oct. 25 2019

Have you ever had an experience in your life that was so incredible that you just couldn't wait to run out and tell somebody? This incredible story that I'm sharing with all of you is that kind of story. As I sit here almost ten years after being released from Kingman State Prison, I'm finally ready to begin writing this book so that my testimony of all the miracles of God that I personally witnessed while serving time at Kingman will be properly recorded and then hopefully published so has to serve as a light of hope to all those who sit in the darkness of despair and hopelessness in prisons and jails around the world.

I'm going to tell it exactly like it happened, as if I were standing at the pulpit of your local Church and sharing my testimony with all of you. So with that let's jump right into this incredible story for the glory of God...Amen

"We have a very special guest with all of us today, His name is Paul Vescio. Paul serves as a Community Chaplain in an Acute Care Center and Rehab in Phoenix Arizona. Chaplain Paul is a Baker, Writer, Published Author and has a very exciting testimony to share with all of us here today. Come on up here Chaplain Paul and welcome to our Church."

"Thank You Pastor, it is an honor being here with all of you today, Thank you for inviting me here so I can share my testimony with all of you."

On December 6 2007, St Nicholas Day, I was arrested in a sting operation in Mesa Arizona. As I pulled up next to an undercover police officer who called himself Joe, my helper got out of the car and handed Joe a ~~once~~ *ounce* of cocaine, at that point Joe gave the signal to move in by shutting the hood of his truck. Then just like in the movies, a white tactical van pulled right behind my car blocking me in as a swarm of police and undercover vehicles came driving in from all directions with two police helicopters flying in from overhead. I placed my hands on the steering wheel and even though an undercover police officer had his firearm pointed right at my head I was as cool as a cucumber. I was at peace knowing that this crazy drug dealing circus that I had been living in for some time was finally over.

I call that day my second adoption because of the grace of God. In October 1962 at two months old I was adopted by my Mother and Father and if Abba Father had not done anything else for me for the rest of my life that one single act of compassion and love in my life would have been enough because I received the best parents ever. They are both with our Lord now and I miss and love them with all my heart. That's the short version of my first adoption, its an incredible story by itself, maybe I'll come back and share it with you all sometime.

The day I was arrested was my second adoption, I was adopted out of a life of crime and adopted into a life of serving Christ our Lord. God basically said that He was sending me to a place where I could learn His word and be brought into a closer relationship with His Son Christ Jesus. I was given a gift of time to be made ready for serving Christ our Lord for the glory of God..

Please use the Blessing pages of this book to write your positive thoughts and blessings of the day. All to often we tend to forget the blessings that God provides to us. As you write and date your thoughts and blessings you can go back and read and share them with family members and receive great peace, hope, strength, and joy. John 14:27

Chaplain Basye's Perfect Rainbow

Before Chaplain Basye was approved as Head Chaplain at Kingman State Prison he got a little frustrated because it was taking some time. One day he asked God in anger as he threw his hammer to the ground, " Lord if I'm going to get this job I need a sign from You." Then he found a shiny penny on the ground and took it as a sign that God would provide for all his needs.

The Body of Christ under Chaplain Eddy invited Chaplain Basye to come to the prison so they could bless and pray over him in asking for God's blessing in approving the job as Head Chaplain at Kingman. As Chaplain Basye and Sandy were turning off of the highway going to the prison a beautiful rainbow appeared right in front of them. Chaplain Basye basically said, " Lord, that was Noah's sign, I need something more than that." Upon arrival at the prison as Chaplain Basye and his wife Sandy were walking through the prison on their way to the Chapel building the Lord's perfect rainbow followed Chaplain Basye every step of the way, then it rested upon the Chapel. Needless to say Chaplain Basye was Arizona's first ex-offender to be approved as Head Chaplain of a prison. The Governor may have had to sign off on it, but it was Abba Father's blessing and love that made it happen Amen... Chaplain Basye arrived at Kingman State Prison just a few short months before I did.

Chapter One
I Have Arrived

On the day of my sentencing two very important men came to speak on my behalf, the first one was the Director of Blood Services for the Red Cross. I had met Scott after 911 happened. I brought cheesecakes down to the Red Cross and gave Scott my Yankee jersey to hang on the wall for inspiration for all those who were giving blood in support of our hurting nation. Afterword I would continue to bring homemade cheesecakes to the Red Cross for the following few years leading up to my arrest. The other man who spoke at my sentencing was the Director of Hospice. I had been donating cheesecakes to Hospice for years and Todd and I became good friends. Both Todd and Scott helped in reducing my sentence from three and a half years to two and a half years. I told the Judge that I take full responsibility for my actions, boy when was the last time we heard a politician say that in this country?

I looked over at my family and I waved goodbye then I was escorted to a holding room and then time stopped. I was sent to Towers Jail and placed in a cell with two other guys. it was brutal. The conditions were pretty bad but we all got along well. We just sat in our cell all day and night and read the Bible and talked about it. Soon or I should say not soon enough I was sent to Alhambra Prison for classification. At that facility, they move inmates around a lot. Inmates are given blood tests and IQ tests and are classified for security. A nonviolent drug offender like myself would be classified for a level 2 or level 3 yard. The more violent the offense the higher the security.

I was eventually sent to a level 2 yard. After Alhambra it was off to Buckeye State Prison. I thought that would be my final stop, thank God, it wasn't. The prison was older and the yards and pods were smaller, please excuses my language but it sucked. I was placed in the back of the pod on the top bunk. I felt like Frankenstein, you know when the mad scientist pulls Frankenstein up to the ceiling with chains? And to make matters worse the evaporator cooler was right above me, it was noisy and hot.

Oh, I almost forgot, I was sentenced on April 30th 2008 and in Arizona that means summer is just about here. I don't know about you but I do not do well in the heat, I like the cold weather much better. I am originally from Stamford Connecticut where it snows in the winter.

The Church service at Buckeye was only once a week and that consisted of a Priest coming in with one or two people and with less than ten inmates showing up for the service. So there I was stuck.

The prison clothing made me hot because it had wax on it. I'm not making this stuff up the pants actually had a wax coating on them. I guess the wax makes them last longer. I don't know. I'm going to have to Google this one. Anyway, there I was sitting on my bunk looking down at the TV below me. The guy on the bunk just below me was watching a show about Navy ships, Suddenly I looked just as a closeup of a battle ship's number was shown on the screen, the ship's number was, 193. I could not believe my eyes, please let me explain. 193 is a very special number for my family. My Aunt lived at 193 and we lived in a condominium at 193 back east in Conn. So when I saw the ship's number, I bowed my head in prayer and asked God to please get me out of there.

"Please, God, bring me to a place that's cooler, please bring me to a place where I can have my own space, and please God, bring to a place where there's a bigger Church."

Then three days later I was rolled up and sent to Kingman State Prison with Nick Martin who was an older man. Nick was sent to prison for having one bottle of expired prescription drugs in his car. Prescription drugs that were in his name. Nick, a grandfather and the nicest guy you could ever meet was given two years in prison for that offense. So be careful out there people.

When I got to Kingman I landed in space number 7, The number seven in the Bible represents, Completion, Perfection, Fullness, Abundance, and

Rest. I did not get an upper or lower bunk in the back of the pod which is usually what happens when new arrivals show up on the yard. The person right next to me was Pastor Jose who was an ordained Pastor and Head Chaplain's Clerk at the time. Pastor Jose placed me under his wing in the Church. Pastor Jose became like a mentor to me. Oh, and has for the temperature in Kingman when I arrived at the end of May. Well a freak winter storm had blown in and because the air conditioners were already turned on it was freezing in the pods. I had to borrow my neighbor's thermal t-shirt to keep warm. The Church at Kingman was on fire at that time. The Church had an army of Pastors and volunteers coming in to help teach Christian programs like, Maximized Manhood, Celebrate Recovery, The Speakers Forum, Bible Studies and more. There were Christian Church Services and programs, Catholic Services, Mormon Services, and even a Jehovah Witness volunteer who visited the prison often..

The praise and worship band that the Christian Church had according to Meadowlark Lemon who came up to preach twice said that the praise and worship band at Kingman was as good as anything he's seen traveling around the world. God had delivered in a big way, He blessed me with three out of three awesome blessings and I give all the praise, glory and honor to Abba Father for His awesome blessings and love in my life...Amen

The Christian Church of Kingman State Prison was structured as follows. There was Head Chaplain

Wayne Basye and Assistant Chaplain Lewis, then there were three Inmate Chaplain's Clerks which included a Head Chaplain's Clerk and two Chaplain's Clerks under him. Then there was a Head Pastor for each of the three yards. The body of Christ also elected through the leadings of the Holy Spirit Pod Pastors for each of the many pods in the prison.

A prison pod is a 53 man open room with rows of beds and upper and lower bunks in the back of the pod. Each pod came with stalls and showers in the back of the pod. Each pod had phones on the wall where inmates could call home provided that they had money on their phone accounts.

When I arrived at Kingman I was a broken man, I was face down in the dirt. I thank God for His blessings and love in lifting me up because otherwise, I would not have been able to make it. The pull of the dark-side is very strong in prison, but thank God when we place our faith, hope, and trust in God He is always faithful to help us along the way.

Like I said I was down for the count. I realized that Abba Father held my loved ones in the palm of His hand and that I could no longer be there for my family to protect and help them. I was beaten, I was done, I was ready to raise the white flag and surrender my life completely to Christ, and that is exactly what I did. I got down on my knees and gave my life to Christ in genuine repentance and love and I thank God every day that I did. Romans 10:9 John3:16

Pastor Jose took me under his wing right from the start. Soon I began going to Church. I got plugged into many programs that the Church of Kingman offered to the inmates. I passed out Christian bookmarks and devotionals. I helped Pastor Jose set up the English Inmate Bible Study that he facilitated once a week. I posted info about Church events and programs on each of the pod doors on the South Yard. Oh, I almost forgot my space number was 2A7. I always thought of it as being 007.

Then on June 22 2008 one month since I arrived at Kingman I along with over fifty other inmates were Baptized by Chaplain Wayne Basye. I'll tell you about this great man of God in Chapter Two. On the day I was baptized I climbed into a square vertical container filled with water then Chaplain Basye asked me if I had truly excepted Christ into my life. I said, "Yes I have." Then he said, "In that case; Paul Vescio, I baptized you in the name of the Father, Son, and Holy Spirit. I dunked under the water then emerged as a new creation in Christ Jesus, old things had passed away all things had become new for the glory of God...

Shortly after that as I was sitting on my bed I looked over at my washcloth and noticed something incredible. Let me explain, there were shelves and a locker with a small shelf to write on at each of the inmate's spaces.

After I shower, I hang my towel and washcloth on the door of my locker to dry. As I was sitting on my bed I noticed an image in my washcloth. I asked Pastor Jose to take a look. What I actually said was,

"Pastor, I do not want to make a federal case about this but can you please take a look at my washcloth and tell me what you see?"

Pastor got up and looked over and said and I quote,

"Oh, that's Jesus." end quote

The face of Christ had revealed itself on my washcloth shortly after I was baptized at Kingman. The washcloth signifies that my sins were washed clean. That meaning is only one of many implications and meanings for this miracle of God. The image was not a stain or paint, it was embedded in the fabric itself and interestingly there were 7 red spots on my washcloth that I sill have in my possession today. Some inmates could see Christ very clearly and still others could not see the image at all. Christ is revealed not recognized. This event is just another example of this truth.

Christ Yeshua Revealed not Recognized The road to Emmaus Luke 24:13-32

There were many times where I was at a low point in prison and when that happened the image on the cloth became more visible to me as in to say, "I am here Paul, it's all going to be Ok." and it worked, I would look at the face of Christ and receive great peace and comfort. One more very interesting note about this miracle, this event was very personal to me. I did not tell many inmates about it. I did not call CNN or Fox News, I wanted to keep this between God and me and whoever God placed on my path to share it with. You have to understand this was very personal and very special to me and it still is to this day. I do not talk about this very often. One last thing, one night while my neighbor was watching TV he invited me to come and watch a documentary about The Shroud of Turin with him, so I decided to go and take a look. I had always been very interested in the shroud so I pulled up a stool and began watching.

At some point they showed a closeup of the image on the shroud and to my shock and utter amazement, the facial expression on the shroud matched the facial expression on my washcloth. As incredible as all of this sounds, it is the truth. And as time went on and I became stronger in the Lord, the image slowly faded away. When I came back home in 2010 I could barely see the image, Now it's gone completely. The seven faded red spots on the cloth remain visible even to this very day. Please don't tell CNN about this, the last thing I want is a thousand people standing in front of my house singing and holding candles; Ok, except for Christmas Eve that is.

Chapter Two
Chaplain Wayne Basye

Chaplain Basye was and still is a huge influence in my life. I spoke to him on the phone this morning he now Pastors a Church in Yucca Arizona. It's now been exactly ten years after I was released from Kingman and this is the year I am finally ready to begin writing this book. What's fascinating about all of this is Chaplain Bayse and Doug are putting on the play that we created in Christmas of 2009. Doug who is my dear brother in Christ was an inmate with me and who eventually became a Chaplain's Clerk and Head Pastor of the North Yard, and you won't believe this but he is now married to Chaplain Basye's sister and serves as an Associate Pastor at the Church in Yucca, unbelievable. While I was in Kingman The Body of Christ put on a Christmas Play called Scrooge a Christmas Carol. God used me to write and direct the play. I even wrote myself a small part in the play singing a song called, Thank You Very Much. Chaplain Basye invited me to come and sing that same song in the play at his Church this Christmas.

Where to start when describing a mighty man of God like Chaplain Basye? How about at the beginning as I remember it being told by Chaplain Basye himself at Church service. This is just a small portion of his incredible testimony.

Chaplain Wayne Basye served in the United States Marines as a Marine Corps Sergeant in Vietnam. He told us that one time while walking through the jungle the enemy threw a grenade at him and it rolled and blew up right underneath him. He was blown in the air and landed on the ground with only minor cuts. Sometime later he was told by a doctor that, that incident caused Chaplain Basye to have the same effect as a vasectomy and he could not have children. Chaplain Basye would share stories like that one in showing God's grace in his life. God protected him knowing that one day he would serve as Chaplain and as Pastor in leading many people to Christ for the glory of God.

Chaplain Basye was a very good family man and a very successful Contractor and he still is, but he became a drug user back in the day and by his own words said he wasn't very good at it. He wore a cowboy hat and stuck out like a sore thumb. I think he lived in Long Beach at the time and all the drug dealers just looked at him and shook their heads. They didn't rob him because they figured that the Chaplain would be giving them his money for their drugs anyway.

Oh, I almost forgot, Chaplain Basye was and still is a seasoned musician. He writes his own music and plays the guitar and was key in creating the praise and worship team at Kingman. Chaplain Basye arrived at Kingman only a few months prior to my arrival. God was setting the stage for a mighty harvest at that prison.

Back in the 1980s Chaplain Basye was arrested and released and during his release before sentencing his girlfriend talked him into partying one last time so they did some cocaine and stayed up all night. The next morning his girlfriend took off and Chaplain Basye decided to go and have breakfast at a CoCo's. He was planning to do a dine and dash so he sat by the front door. After he ate his food he noticed that the cash register was open and that the customer who was at the register paid with a hundred dollar bill. Chaplain Basye took hold of a steak knife that was on his table and stood up and told the manager who was behind the register to hand over the cash. The manager who was a woman gave him the money then the manager and the busboy ran after Chaplain Basye. When they caught up with him Chaplain Basye pulled the steak knife on them and told them to back off.

They ran back to the restaurant and called the police. This CoCo's was located in a residential neighborhood and what happened next was something straight out of the movies. Chaplain Basye could see the police helicopter lifting off from the ground because the police station was right down the street. Then the cops showed up on scene.

By this time there were many people gathering around to see what was going on, so Chaplain Basye decided to just blend into the crowd and play it cool. Well, when a police car pulled up and the officer got out of the car, Chaplain Basye actually walked over to him and asked, "What's going on?"

Then the police helicopter pilot radioed down to the police officer,

"That's the guy!!! He was just standing right next to you."

After seeing that the jig was up and that the cops were now on to him, Chaplain Basye illegally entered into a house with a family of three and held them hostage at knifepoint. Then the S.W.A.T. Team was called in and all hell was about to break loose.

What happened next is just another example of how God protects those who will one day be a shining example of his grace and love. Chaplain Basye was standing in the living room as a man and his wife and young son were being held against their will at knifepoint. The S.W.A.T. Team Sniper gave the signal that he had his target. The sniper was about to shoot Chaplain Basye in the head when the young boy looked him in the eyes and said,

"You're not going to hurt us are you mister?"

Chaplain Basye looked into the young boy's eyes then realized that deep down he was not that kind of person. Then just has the sniper was about to pull the trigger Chaplain Basye said,

"No son; I'm not going to hurt anyone." and with that he dropped the knife hitting the coffee table, damaging it, and causing Chaplain Basye to receive an additional charge of criminal damage on top of the other fifteen charges that he committed that faithful day. Now watch this; right as the knife left the Chaplain's hand the S.W.A.T. Team Commander radioed to the sniper telling him to stand down, stand down, the suspect dropped the weapon.

Chaplain Basye was arrested and charged with armed robbery, kidnapping, and a whole lot of other charges to boot. He was then taken into custody and booked into the LA Jail and placed in a single cell right across from the night stalker, Richard Ramirez. Soon after Chaplain Basye was moved to a pod-like cell and one day he decided to end his life. The Chaplain began asking the other inmates if they had a razor blade so that he could go to the back of the pod and end his life but God had other plans that faithful day.

Chaplain Basye asked a few inmates for a blade with no luck, then he went back to his bunk. About that time a voice from above asked Chaplain Basye to say this prayer. The guy on the bunk just above Chaplain Basye said,

"Wayne, say this prayer, Wayne, say this prayer."

The guy did not give up, he kept asking Chaplain Basye to say a certain prayer. Chaplain Basye looked up at the guy and said,

"Look, if you give me a blade I'll say your stupid prayer."

The man handed Chaplain Basye a blade then said,

"Ok, Wayne, now bow your head and repeat after me."

Chaplain Basye bowed his head and said the Prayer of Salvation, then the Holy Spirit came upon him like a flood and he began to cry and suddenly Chaplain Basye was born again of the Spirit of God. One minute he was an unbeliever then after he had said the prayer he was suddenly changed for the glory of God.

Hebrews 11:1 Now faith is the substance of things hoped for that evidence of things not seen. For all those who are seeking proof of the existence of God all one has to do is ask a believer in Christ Yeshua to please share their testimony with you. Praise God that Chaplain Basye had become born again because if this had never happened thousands of people out there would still be lost. I firmly believe that one life has the power to effect many in a negative or positive way. Upon seeing that the Chaplain was now born again the man who had shared the prayer began shouting "PRAISE GOD HALLELUYAH!!!" Then he sliced his toe on the edge of the bunk and it began bleeding all over the place. The man was taken way and Chaplain Basye never saw him again, to this day he believes that the man was a messenger of God sent to lead him to Christ.

Chaplain Basye has a musical CD of his incredible testimony, I hope to one day give it out with this book, we will see.

Now I'm going to fast forward to when Chaplain Basye and his wife Sandy came to Kingman Az. Chaplain Basye and Sandy moved to Kingman Arizona and by that time they both had years of Prison Ministry under their belts. One day as Sandy was looking on the computer she noticed that there was a prison close by so why not volunteer there in sharing the love of Christ.

The Chaplain called the prison and Chaplain Eddie answered the phone, well one thing led to another and because of the Chaplain's references in describing him as being a very faithful man of God, Chaplain Eddie said to Chaplain Basye,

"I think I just found my replacement."

Chaplain Basye soon became the first ex-offender to be hired as Head Chaplain in the Arizona Prison System. Brown Cards are not needed in the State of Arizona in order to serve in the prison system but in California Brown Cards were required. Here is a little side story about Chaplain Basye needing a Brown Card back in the day. The Basyes did not have a reliable car to drive and without a brown card they needed an escort every time they went to the prison. Chaplain Basye needed a brown card. So a Pastor friend who also served in the prison system had to escort the Basyes into the prison every time they went. Now this became somewhat of an inconvenience for the Pastor so one night the Pastor said this prayer with the Basyes,

"Lord, Chaplain Basye needs a brown card, Now Lord the Basyes are doing Your will and they need a break, so how about helping them out a little? Amen"

Soon after as Chaplain Basye was entering the prison, the secretary looked at him and said,

"Chaplain, I don't know how you did this but here's your brown card."

The State of Arizona does not hire ex-offenders to work as Chaplains in the prison system, well that was until God got involved with things and Chaplain Basye became the first ex-offender to be hired as a Chaplain working for D.O.C. All things are possible when we place our faith and trust in Christ Jesus...Amen

I got one more quick story to tell you before we get back to my testimony. Back in the day while still living in California, Chaplain Basye had gotten his brown card but there was still the issue of a reliable car to get the Basyes back and forth to the prison. Well, that same Pastor asked God to help get the Basyes a good running car or truck and shortly after that prayer of faith. Chaplain Basye was working on this woman's house at the time. You see Chaplain Basye is a very successful contractor. He built the Church building in Yucca that he now Pastors. The woman whose house the Chaplain was working on had a van for sale that she was asking seventeen grand for.

The Chaplain offered to trade the remodeling job on her house for the van, the woman agreed. Then after the job was completed the woman paid the Chaplain for the job and gave him the van as a bonus for free. You've got to love a story like that, I know I do. When things like that happen in a person's life they have two options, either chalk it up as a total coincidence or realize that something greater is at work in our lives. After all the things that I have personally witnessed at Kingman, I know without a shadow of a doubt that there is a living God Who controls all things... I will most likely be repeating that statement many times throughout this book...

Chaplain Basye personally witnessed so many miracles during his time at Kingman Prison that if he sat down and wrote a book about them it would no doubt be twice the size of this one. The most significant Miracles of God at Kingman State Prison were in the countless number of inmates who gave their lives to Christ while Chaplain Basye and Sandy were there. Thank You Chaplain Basye and Sandy for all of your kindness, love, and support. I would not be the kind of Community Chaplain of God I am today without the positive influence that you both had on my life... John 14:27

My Blessings

Chapter Three
A Basket of Miracles

I think I'm going to really like writing this chapter because when I tell these stories I get lit on fire for the Lord. The Bible says in Revelation12:11, And they overcame him by the blood of the lamb and by the word of their testimony and they did not love their lives to the death.

One of the meanings of this Scripture verse is, we overcame satan when we share our testimony with others. We know what we had witnessed in our lives is absolutely true and satan has no power in trying to create any doubt in our minds about it. Our testimonies of Christ's power and love in our lives is one of the Spiritual Weapons of choice in defeating the powers of darkness.

When I first arrived at Kingman I had not spoken to my family in over two weeks, that's because inmates need to have a phone account set up to call home. A phone account is where a family member places money in an account like a prepaid system. Every time an inmate calls home it costs five dollars. Each call is for about fifteen minutes long, so five dollars can add up real quick. I called home only once or twice a week, mostly once a week. I decided to go see the counselor to set up my phone account. Please let me first explain. Some of the counselors in the prison system keep banker's hours. They were never around and when they were in their office they had a tendency to play games with the inmates. Like making us wait in long lines for hours at a time and just when you think you are going to be lucky enough to actually see them they lock up shop and go home for the day. So I was expecting the same old runaround when I paid my counselor a visit, but to my shocking surprise there was no line, and even more incredible the door was opened, so I walked in and introduced myself. My counselor informed me about how to set up my phone account and about a few other issues I had. All in all, I was there for about forty minutes, then I got up to leave and as I opened the door an inmate letter fell to the floor, now I had a choice, I could either leave it be or I could pick it up and bring it to my counselor.

Here is the layout of the place. There were three counselor's offices and a short hallway leading to the door out. Where I was standing the counselor could not see me. I thought to myself, this guy is a nice guy, so I bent over and right when I touched the inmate letter my counselor' called out, "Hey Paul, come here."

Now I thought that he saw me pick up the letter but he couldn't. I walked back into his office and without saying a word, he had the phone extended towards me in his hand. I walked over, took the phone from his hand and said, "hello."

It was my girlfriend she called at the exact moment and the exact time that I was in the counselor's office. She was screaming and crying,

"OMG!!!OMG!!! ARE YOU ALL RIGHT? ARE YOU ALL RIGHT?!!!!!!!

She was crying, you see her and my family had not heard from me in a couple of weeks because the prison system moves inmates around at first for classification. My counselor told me, that had only happened one other time since he started working at that prison, where the inmate was in his office when the family member called. Let me break this down a bit. If I did not pick up that inmate letter and said to myself screw this guy and walked out the door he would have told my girlfriend that I had just left. If the inmate letter was not in the door in the first place I would have missed the call. If my girlfriend did not call at the exact time that she did she would have missed being able to talk to me.

As I write this even now I am amazed of what actually took place that faithful day. All of the things that made this miracle happen had to be in perfect alignment, that's what makes this a miracle. God's timing is always perfect and He is always in control. Remember, there were no long lines waiting to see the counselor, in fact there were no lines at all. That alone is unheard of in prison. The door was unlocked and open. The counselor was in his office, the inmate letter was in the door. That one

act of kindness in reaching down to bring the counselor that letter was a key element in all of this.
Never understatement the power of a small act of
kindness in the world, this story is living proof of
that truth.

One day as I was walking through the south yard
on my way to the chow hall, I began musing with
God. I started saying,

"Lord, I'd like a cheese danish, how come I can't
have a cheese danish Lord? Everyone else gets a
cheese danish. I would really like a cheese danish
Lord."

Later that same day as I was standing at my
space in the pod my neighbor John came in with a
kid helping him carry two boxes of stuff. I asked
him what was going on. John said that the items in
the boxes were from Sam's Club. Every once in a
while the prison would run a fundraiser where inmates were given the opportunity to buy things that
were not usually offered in prison.

John was a level three and that means he could
work outside of the prison. John worked on the
trailers outside of the prison. Being a level three
also means that he could buy as much stuff as he
could afford. I was a level two. Level one has the
least privileges, level threes have the most privileges.

So there I was standing by my bunk watching as
John began unpacking his boxes of Sam's Club
stuff, then he reaches down grabs one item and
tosses it on my bunk. That one item was a cheese

danish. Thank You Lord. Now, for all of you who may say, "Well, John must have heard you talking about wanting a cheese danish." Sorry, John was not at the prison at the time I was walking to the chow hall and I was walking by myself. No one heard me ask God for a cheese danish. So it clearly looks like something out of the ordinary happened here. Now how about a few more stories like this one just for fun?

Just a side note. I'm sharing these stories with you not to brag or boast but to present the evidence of things not seen, as in, the evidence that there is something far greater Who's working in all of our lives. Hebrews 11:1

One day as I was standing by my bunk, I noticed that Pastor Jose had an empty cup of rocky road ice cream that he was using to hold his pens and pencils in. As I was standing there I did it again, I started saying,

"Lord, I'd like some ice cream like that, how come I can't have ice cream like that? Lord, I would really like to have some ice cream like that."

Now what I am about to tell you is the God's honest truth. Later that same day I walked over to the Chapel. The Chapel was not a traditional Church building like you may be thinking. The Chapel at Kingman was an all purposes room. The Chapel was just a big room with a stage and rows of chairs. As I entered the Chapel there was something going on. One of my Brothers in Christ asked

me to please stay for the Speaker's Forum Graduation because the North Yard was closed and the inmates who were graduating couldn't have any
guests. My Brothers in Christ were asking inmates
to please stay for the graduation so that more people would be there.

I did not know what the Speaker's Form was at
the time. The Speaker's Forum was a seven-man
class that teaches believers in Christ how to relate
things around us to the Bible. I would go on to one
day graduate this awesome teaching. So there I was
sitting in the front row watching as the graduation
unfolded, then at its conclusion, I stood up and
turned around and to my surprise there sitting on
the table was four gallons of ice cream and choco-
late cake. My plate was full.

Thank You Lord for blessing number two, now
it's off to blessing number three.

One day as I was walking to chow I heard over
the loudspeaker,

"Movie night, it's movie night and popcorn for
all level threes."

Well, I was a level two and could not go to
movie night, I did not have that privileged, so I began asking God,

"Lord, I would like to see a movie, how come I
can't see a movie Lord? Lord, I would really like to
see a movie."

Then I thought to myself, which movie would I
like to see? Either The Passion of Christ or Jesus of

Nazareth, so I chose Jesus of Nazareth and said,

"Yes, I would like to see Jesus of Nazareth Lord."

After chow on that same day as I was leaving the chow hall I looked over and noticed that a few of my Brothers in Christ were sitting on the sidewalk over by the Chapel, so I walked over and asked them what was going on. They told me that the Chaplain had gone home early that day and that we were going to see a movie that night. I asked them what move are we going to see?

"Jesus of Nazareth"

Thank You Lord.

I had asked God for new deck shoes because mine were worn out. In prison it takes a while to get new clothes. One day as I was waiting by the gate a guy whom I did not know walks over to me and asked me if I wanted new deck shoes. I looked at him and asked,

"What size deck shoes are they?

He said that they were size 8, that's my size. The guy gave them to me for free. Thank You Lord for all of Your awesome blessings and love...Amen

Do you like pizza? Who doesn't right? Here's a little story about a Bible Study and a Little Caesar's Pizza Guy. We did a Bible Study every day out on the yard for about an hour just before lunchtime. There were five of us in the study. The Bible Study was led by a guy who went by the name Red Neck, his real name was Keith. One day as I was walking to chow I started doing it again, I began asking God for a pizza, now the pizza at chow was good but nothing like a real pizza on the outside.

"Lord, I would really like a pizza, how come I can't have a pizza Lord? Lord, I would really like a pizza."

The next day Red Neck came walking in my pod and handed me a Little Caesar's Pizza, he told me to share it with the other guys who were in the Bible Study. I cut out the Little Caesar's dude on the box and I still have it to this day.

"LORD YOU'VE DONE IT AGAIN!!!!!!!"

Where did the pizza come from, you must be asking? It came from a fundraiser like the Sam's Club Fundraiser. Very cool.

I started a book of blessings where I would write down my blessings, I highly recommend that people make one of their own. A book of blessings is very powerful in lifting up our spirits when we are feeling low.

By writing down and dating our blessings we are reminded of God's love and of His workings in our lives. We draw great strength and hope when we go back and read about all the blessings that we have received in the past. All too often as time passes we tend to forget the small meaningful blessings of God in our lives.

Here is one more blessing for the road. While I was in prison I found out about a woman who's ministry it was in providing Bibles to inmates. All one had to do was to write her a letter telling her about their walk with Christ and what being a Christian means to them. I wrote her a letter and on Christmas Eve 2008 I received a Family Foundations Family Bible. I received a second Bible on Easter. The second one was given to me by Bobby who was my Brother in Christ at Kingman. I would one day write letters to that same woman in helping members of the Body of Christ at Kingman receive Bibles.

Chapter Four
A Hedge of Protection

The stories in this chapter are going to be about the protective covering that God placed over me while I was an inmate at Kingman. First, it is unheard of for an inmate in prison not to have been in a fight or have been in some kind of dangerous situation. In the time that I served at Kingman State Prison, I was untouched. God had placed a hedge of protection over me.

Any threat or anyone who was even rude to me was either rolled up and removed from the prison or their attitudes were suddenly changed or God placed inmates around me to protect me from being in harm's way. Here are a few of the many stories about God's hedge of protection in my life while I was at Kingman.

The Body of Christ at Kingman were taught to be kind, helpful, humble, compassionate servants of Christ. We were the light of Christ in what otherwise was a very dark and depressing place. As we go about our day we greet inmates in passing by saying things like, good morning, God bless you, have a blessed day and so forth.

One day as I was standing in the line at chow, I

looked over at a guy who was right next to me and said,

"Something is telling me to say God bless you."

What I said came out kind of wrong.

The guy was a very serious inmate and a very dangerous individual, believe me when I tell you this kind of guy you do not want to piss off. He looked back at me and said,

"Well, something is telling me to tell you to go to hell."

I apologized and said that I meant no disrespect. Then a short time later that same man was rolled up and moved off of the yard. Another time as I was sitting at Chaplain Lewis' Tuesday afternoon Bible Study at the Chapel, a strange guy whom I had never seen before came in and sat one chair over to my right. Here's the setup. I was sitting in the fourth row from the front, the row had about six or seven chairs in it. The guy was sitting at the end of the row to my right with an empty chair between us. Felix walks in from my left and instead of sitting next to me to my left he crosses past me and sits in-between me and the guy. God was setting things up to protect me and I didn't even know it. As the Bible Study progressed, Chaplain Lewis said this scripture verse,

"And we were equated as sheep to the slaughter all day long."

One of my brothers in Christ who was there that day raised his hand and asked Chaplain Lewis the meaning of that verse. And as Chaplain Lewis began explaining its meaning to all of us, the guy to my right suddenly stood up and punched Felix right in the eye. Felix was a big guy. After he was hit he fell backward then defended himself, at this point the guards came rushing in and took both of them away. Felix did not get any charges. It's prison protocol that both inmates be restrained until an investigation about the incident is completed.

If I had taken a hit like Felix received, I most likely would have been knocked out or worse. I believe God placed Felix in between me and that guy to protect me from being hurt.

We found out later that the guy who hit Felix was on psych meds and was freaking out because he wanted to be removed from the yard. When an inmate feels that their life is at risk or when an inmate racks up a huge gambling, drug or store debt they'll purposely get into a fight so that the prison will move them to another facility. This is why prison is so dangerous because if you are that unlucky person who another inmate chooses to beat the hell out of just so they can be moved to a different prison then you could wind up in the hospital or worse. God had placed Felix in my life to protect me, He did it automatically. Felix took a very hard punch to his eye that day and he did not get a black eye or get hurt very badly, that alone is a small miracle. Thank You Abba Father for Your hedge of protection that day, even now I am forever grateful for Your blessings and love in my life.

This next story is yet another example of God's hedge of protection at Kingman. One time as I was leaving the chow hall heading back to my pod a guard stopped me at the gate and pointed to my shirt and asked,

"Where's your ID Vescio?"

I looked down at my shirt and said.

"I don't know, I guess I left it at my space, can I please go and look?"

"Go, hurry up"

I ran back to my bunk and I found my ID laying on the floor, it must have dropped off. You have to understand, if I get written up for this it could jeopardize my 1291 early release. Senate Bill 1291 was a 90 day early release for inmates who were first time, nonviolent, non-repetitive, drug offenders. If an inmate who qualifies for a 1291 gets a ticket, the prison board could take that early release away from the inmate. So there was a lot at stake for me here. As I was walking back to the gate with my ID Anthony came walking on by. I asked him to please take my ID to the chow hall and drop it on the floor so that I could go in there and find it and not get a ticket. Anthony was stopped at the gate and came walking back to me. He handed me my ID and said,

"Here, don't worry about it, just tell them the truth."

At this point I looked up to the sky and said,

"Lord, I place my trust in You concerning this issue."

Then I walked up to the guard and said,

"Sir, I must have dropped my ID at my space before I went to chow. I'm sorry, am I going to get a ticket for this?"

Just then the lieutenant who was standing right next to the guard turned his back on me, then the guard looked at me and said,

"Well, I guess the lieutenant didn't see anything so I guess you're good."

I could not believe what just happened. I walked back to my bunk thanking and praising God. I will say, this story is only just one of a few very similar situations while I was there. Now that I think of it here are two more hedge of protection stories that I can share with you.

One time while I was at Kingman a riot almost broke out because the air-conditioners were turned off to early in the year. In Kingman Arizona it gets cooler in the fall but sometimes it heats up again during the month of October. That is exactly what happened in 2009. The temperature heated up and the prison had already turned off the AC for the Fall and Winter months. As the pods got hotter so did the inmates, and one day it reached a boiling point. The inmates started protesting by standing out on all three yards as the Heads entered into negotiations with the prison authority. As night set in all hell was about to let loose at the prison. The

Body of Christ prayed our hearts out for God's intervention in this matter. This was a very serious situation, if a full blown riot broke out at the prison many inmates could get hurt or even killed. The end result was God had answered our prayers and the situation was resolved, there was some minor damage by a few lone youngsters who thought they were being cool, but thank God no one was hurt. Thank You Abba Father for Your hedge of protection concerning this matter...Amen

During the spring and summer months it gets very hot in Kingman. I noticed that there was a long line at medical. Inmates needing medicine were forced to stand in a long line outside waiting to be given their meds. And to make matters worse the water fountain outside of pill drop was broken and only had warm water coming out of it.

I also noticed that the big orange coolers on each of the yards that were filled with ice would quickly run out of cool water and run dry. So I organized a prison water and ice protest.

I asked all my brothers in Christ along with other inmates to please write inmate letters to the powers that be at Kingman Prison in demanding more ice and cool water for the inmates who had to stand in line at medical and at lunch time chow. Just a side note, there were over three hundred men standing in a single line waiting for chow that moved at a snail's pace each day. During the summer months men were passing out because of the extreme heat of the day during lunchtime.

Well, the Prison Supervisor got wind of who was running the water and ice show and my space was searched on more than one occasion. They could have made my stay there very hard on me because of all of this but God was in full control. The outcome was, there were more water and ice cooler fillings on each yard and inmates who stood in line could now bring their own bottles of water. The only thing that wasn't fixed was the water cooler by medical, but two out of three of our demands were honored and that's not bad at all where prison is concerned.

It's a three hour drive from Phoenix to Kingman so having my family drive all that way just for an hour visit than face a three hour drive back home was a waste as far as I was concerned, so we waited over a year before they came up for a visit. By that time I was a level two and could have a two hour visit. On the second visit I was studying Hebrews 11:1 Which reads, Now faith is the substance of things hoped for the evidence of things not seen.

We do not see Abba Father, The Holy Spirit or Christ Yeshua in the flesh but we see the evidence of their handy work all around us each day in our lives. I wanted to show an example of this truth to my family when I visited with them the day they came up. Boy did I get a chance in a big way to do just that.

As I was sitting with my family I had to go to the rest room so I got up, walked over to the rest room and shut the door and out of reflex I locked the door. As I was taking a leak I heard keys unlocking the door and the guard suddenly bursts in and grabs me and says,

"Your visit is over Vescio you're getting a ticket and getting stripped searched."

I didn't know what was going on, but remained relatively calm. I was taken to a side room. let me explain why this happened in the first place. This was only my second visit at the visitation hall. I had never used the restroom or was ever told the rules. There were two restrooms, one for the visitors with a door and one for the inmates without a door so that the guards could make sure that no contraband was smuggled into the prison. This issue placed my 1291 early release at risk.

At this point I prayed to God for His divine guidance and help in this situation, then I looked the guard right in the eye and said,

"Can I appeal this?"

The guard looked at me, then went to get the sergeant. Now first of all I do not know where that came from. I did not know I could appeal anything in prison. As the guard was getting the sergeant I started praying my heart out saying,

"Holy Spirit please speak through me to resolve this issue, Holy Spirit please speak through me to resolve this situation."

Then when the sergeant came over to talk to me, I looked her right in the eye and without skipping a beat said.

"Mam, my name is Paul Vescio, I'm a Pastor on the south yard, my integrity is without question, if you have any doubt ask Chaplain Basye"

The sergeant looked at me and said,

"Well, Ok Paul, we'll just call this one a warning, you can go back to your visit."

As I sit here and write this story ten years later, even now I am still amazed about what actually took place that faithful day. Needless to say when I returned to my visit that day I had the perfect comparison to Hebrews 11:1 having just lived through it less than two minutes prior.

Matthew 10:19-20

But when they arrest you, do not worry about what to say or how to say it. At that time you will be given what to say, for it will not be you speaking, but the Spirit of your Father speaking through you.

Matthew 10:19-20 happened to me just like it says in the Bible and not just once in my life but many times over the past few years. When real life experiences happen in our lives that match or mirror those in the Bible it strengthens our faith and reinforces and proves that what is written in the Bible is true. Experiences like these strengthen our faith, gives us hope and light us up and we become on fire for the Lord..

Thank You Abba Father, Thank You, Thank You, Thank You...Amen

Chapter Five
Noah and a Perfect Rainbow

Pastor Jose suddenly left on a shift change and was sent to a prison in Oklahoma. I was heartbroken. Pastor Jose was my mentor and friend, he helped to lift me up while I was at Kingman. Pastor Jose had to leave so that I could mature and grow in my walk with Christ. His departure would make me the new Pod Pastor and I excepted that position with honor. I soon created a medicine chest at my bunk where inmates could come for medicine and prayer. I would buy basic cold medicine from store and have it available for those who were sick. In time I would encourage others in the Body of Christ to donate cold medicine from store. I also organized members of the Body of Christ to build Prayer Boxes for every pod in the prison. Gabriel who was my Brother in Christ built and painted beautiful hand made Prayer Boxes. I brought four of them home with me, I gave one to the Activities Director where I serve as a Community Chaplain. After Pastor Jose left I prayed every day that God would place a good person next to me in my pod. The last thing a person wants in prison is for the guy next to them to be a jerk. I had asked God to either place Brian or John Paul next to me. John Paul was the praise and worship drummer in the band. Three days later as I was sleeping, I awoke to see John Paul moving in right next to me at Pastor Jose's old space. I pulled the blanket over my head and started thanking God for placing John Paul next to me. Believe me, getting a good neighbor in prison was like getting a gold nugget. Now, as I was thanking God I heard Him speak to me audibly, Abba Father said,

"Only through hardship can come creation."

Now, I do not have the intellect to come up wi th a statement like that. Think about what's being said here. Only through hardship can come creation. All creation is a product of hardship. The earth was without form and void and darkness was on the face of the deep. Geneses 1:2 Hardship, then came creation. Nine months of pregnancy is hardship then comes creation. Twelve to fifteen years of schooling is hardship, then comes creation. A seed is planted in the ground, hardship, then one day sprouts and begins to grow and eventually blooms and bears fruit for the glory of God, creation. Winter is hardship then comes the Spring and the creation of new life. And lastly, only through the hardship of prison could I have ever become the Community Chaplain of God that I am today. Honestly, I could write a whole book on this one statement alone.

This was not the first time that I had heard the

voice of Abba Father audibly. When I was five years old I awoke to hear the voice of Abba Father calling my name,

"Paulie, Paulie,"

I was very scared, I jumped right out of bed and ran to the stairs, just then at the same time my Father and Mother were coming up the stairs, I turned the corner and in seeing my Father I leaped off of the top step and flew into his arms. At 57 years old I remember it like it was yesterday. This is exactly what we as believers in Christ Yeshua are to do each day when we wake up in the morning, We are to jump right out of bed then run to Abba Father and leap right into His loving Arms. First Samuel 3:2-18 has similarities to what happened to me when I was five years old.

A short time later John Paul was looking through some of the pictures that he had and one of them caught my eye. I asked him to stop and please let me look at the picture that I saw. He handed it to me. It was a picture of a beautiful mountain sunrise. It was the date on the picture that caught my eye. The date on the picture was December 6 2007, the exact day that I was arrested on, or I should say, the day I was adopted into the Family of God. December 6 2007 was the day of my second adoption. Even more fascinating when I turned the picture over the words written on the back read, Big Bug Mesa. That was the name of the mountain range of the picture. Now check this out. I was busted by a sting operation in Mesa Arizona on the same day that the picture was taken. I still have that picture in my possession to this day.

One day as John Paul was walking out onto the yard a wild gray ring-necked dove flew in from out of the desert and landed on his shoulder. Then that same bird and its mate came every morning to our little Bible Study. The Bible Study we did out on the South Yard each morning right before lunch. I named the bird that landed on John Paul's shoulder Noah. Every day for about a month those two doves visited our little Bible Study. These birds were totally tame, we could pet them, hold them, and feed them. It was nothing like I had ever seen in my life. I ask you when was the last time you heard of a wild bird landing on anyone? Now those two birds could have gone to any other part of the prison for food and water but they chose our Bible Study. What a blessing it was to have those two doves walking on the table right in front of us as we were reading the Word of God each morning.

A dove is a bird of peace and love, Abba Father sent those two birds because He was very pleased with our little Bible Study. Our Bible Study was a little light of hope in what otherwise was a very dark and depressing place. The dove story is one of my favorite stories to tell people; it was like a wonderful dream within the nightmare of prison everyday life. Matthew 3:16 b The Spirit of God descending like a dove and alighting upon him.

Genesis 8:10-11

He waited seven more days and again sent out the dove from the ark. When the dove returned to him in the evening, there in its beak was a freshly plucked olive leaf! Then Noah knew that the water had receded from the earth.

There were other kinds of birds that visited us at Kingman. One time as I was walking out on the yard I heard a honking sound coming from above, I looked up and just then a flock of Geese flew over the prison in a perfect V. Another time right before I was released in 2010 a flock of seagulls flew in for a two week visit. I could not believe my eyes.

I'm originally Stamford Connecticut which is located off of Long Island Sound. The seagulls back where I'm from will hover over you and catch pieces of bread in mid air. Sometimes seagulls will swoop down and grab food right out of your hand. I thought that seeing seagulls in the Arizona desert was very cool.

One time as I was standing out in the yard with a few other inmates, a brown sparrow flew a wide circle waist high around me and another inmate. the sparrow flew around us three times before flying off.

Matthew 10:29-31

Are not two sparrows sold for a penny? Yet not one of them will fall to the ground outside your Father's care. And even the very hairs on your head are all numbered. So don't be afraid; you are worth more than many sparrows.

One day as I was sitting at my space writing, Joe who was the head of the pod for the whites said.

"Pastor Paul we have two new arrivals today."

I turned around and to my shocking surprise one of the guys was my friend Jimmy. Jimmy was a friend of mine whom I had known for a number of years. Jimmy was first sent to the back of the pod and placed in an upper and lower bunk.. something that I had thankfully avoided, Thank You Abba Father.

At first I thought Jimmy might be a plant. I mean this was to coincidental. I began thinking old school, street smarts kinda way concerning Jimmy. I had to be very careful. If he was a plant and I slipped and admitted to doing something illegal in my past I could receive more time and Jimmy could receive less time for snitching on me. My whole thinking about all of this was totally wrong. At some point I had a heart to heart with Jimmy and he assured me that he was more worried about me than I was about him. You see Jimmy's father was in charge of all the prisons in Arizona back in the day and if the other inmates got wind of that information it could place Jimmy's life in jeopardy. After our little talk I realized that Abba Father had placed Jimmy in My Pod to watch over me and that is exactly what he did. In time Jimmy would be moved and placed in the space right behind me.

Jimmy got me out of a few jams in prison and he helped build Prayer Boxes, he also made the only YoYo in Kingman State Prison history. I had asked him to please make me a blue YoYo and I still have it to this day. Jimmy also kept an eye on my space while I was away making sure no one stole or planted anything.

I guess this story should have gone in the last chapter. It's all good.

What would a story about a dove named Noah be without a rainbow in it? So here we go. This story is very hard for me to talk about. I almost changed some of the details of this story, like instead of talking about my son I was going to change it up a bit and say I was in debt with a debtor.

I had a relationship with a woman back in the day and she became pregnant and my son was born. We both agreed to keep it out of the courts. I wanted to do the right thing, well that is after I treated her very poorly and for that I am forever sorry. I wanted to pay more than what we had agreed on for child support. I paid for extra things as well. I have never seen my son. I know that seems terrible and it is, but because of the activities that I was involved in back in the day I do not blame my son's mother for her decision in not letting me see my son. There is not a day that goes by where I do not think about all of this.

Now, before I went to prison I paid a years

worth of child support in advance, then a year later I began freaking out just a bit. You see I was convinced that I would be dragged into court and be forced to deal with the fact I could no longer pay child support.

As 2009 quickly approached, I got more and more concerned about all of this. I could not contact my son's mother by mail because as a prison inmate my info had to be written on each envelope being mailed. My son's mother asked me not to contact her because she did not want her mother to know that I was in prison. So began my slow meltdown about this mess.

As all of this was going on my Brothers in Christ kept telling me to give it to God, just give it to God. At the time I did not understand the concept of giving your problems to God. How do you give a problem to God? I mean we can pray all we want but we still have to row the boat to shore, right? Then one day as I was talking to Bobby my Brother in Christ, I asked him,

"Bobby, how do I give this problem to God, I mean we can pray all we want but we still have to row the boat to shore, right?"

Bobby looked at me and said, "Well just step out of the boat."

"What do you mean, just step out of the boat?"

"Peter stepped out of the boat in faith and walked on water to Jesus."

And with that I began to understand.

Matthew 14:22-33 Jesus Walks on the Water

Immediately Jesus made the disciples get into the boat and go on ahead of him to the other side, while he dismissed the crowd. After he had dismissed them, he went up on a mountainside by himself to pray. Later that night, he was there alone, and the boat was already a considerable distance from land, buffeted by the waves because the wind was against it.

Shortly before dawn Jesus went out to them, walking on the lake. When the disciples saw him walking on the lake, they were terrified. "It's a ghost," they said, and cried out in fear.

But Jesus immediately said to them: "Take courage! It is I. Don't be afraid."

"Lord, if it's you," Peter replied, "tell me to come to you on the water."

"Come," he said.

Then Peter got down out of the boat, walked on the water and came toward Jesus. But when he saw the wind, he was afraid and, beginning to sink, cried out, "Lord, save me!"

Immediately Jesus reached out his hand and caught him. "You of little faith," he said, "why did you doubt?"

And when they climbed into the boat, the wind died down. Then those who were in the boat worshiped him, saying, "Truly you are the Son of God."

When we give something to God think of it this way. Let's say you get a flat tire, you get out of the car upset, you drop lug-nuts, you get very angry, you get hurt, and changing the tire takes twice as long. Now let's give this problem to God. You get a flat tire and before you get out of your car and begin changing the tire you pray for God's guidance, protection, peace, and love in this situation. You ask God for calmness and patience. Then you get out of your car and begin changing the tire in a Godly manner at peace. One way is of the flesh and the other way is of the Spirit.

These are the kind of life lessons we learn from the teachings of God through our walk with Christ. I did manage to get a letter to my son's mother explaining my situation; I did not expect to hear back from her. Then about two weeks later I received a letter from her. in the letter she realized that I was in prison and could no longer afford to pay child support while I was there.

I do not want to get into specifics about the contents of her letter but I will say this when I opened it and read the first line of what she wrote it looked very bad for me. I fell to my knees praying to God to resolve this issue in a way that glorifies Him. After praying on my knees for a few minutes I reopened the letter and read all of its contents, and yes it may have started out with conviction but it ended with mercy.

I was stunned, I felt as though a thousand pounds had been lifted off of my chest, I got up and slowly walked out of the pod dazed, then as I walked out on to the yard I looked over to my right and just outside of the fence was a beautiful rainbow, I tell you, If the fence wasn't there I could have touched it. I had never seen a full rainbow starting from the ground up like that in my life.

This rainbow appeared on a sunny day with scattered clouds in the sky, it was a full rainbow that started from the ground up not more than twenty feet away from me. I could see the whole thing and where it hit the ground on the other side of the valley. This rainbow was an awesome sight to see. It shot across Golden Valley and the pot of gold at the end of the rainbow was now in my heart because of Abba Father's love...

Genesis 9:12-17 And God said, "This is the sign of the covenant I am making between me and you and every living creature with you, a covenant for all generations to come: I have set my rainbow in the clouds, and it will be the sign of the covenant between me and the earth. Whenever I bring clouds over the earth and the rainbow appears in the clouds, I will remember my covenant between me and you and all living creatures of every kind. Never again will the waters become a flood to destroy all life. Whenever the rainbow appears in the clouds, I will see it and remember the everlasting covenant between God and all living creatures of every kind on the earth."

So God said to Noah, "This is the sign of the

covenant I have established between me and all life on the earth."

When we give it all to Abba Father, He is always faithful in helping each of us to get safely through the storm...

My Blessings

Chapter Six
Prayer and the Laying of Hands

In the time that I was at Kingman I personally witnessed people being healed of diabetes, Hep-C, cancer, and many other illnesses, I witnessed relationships restored, money sent to inmates seemingly from out of nowhere, all by the power of prayer and by the laying of hands by the Body of Christ at Kingman State Prison. Here are a few of those stories.

Pops was an older man who was a seasoned musician. Pops played the keyboard along with a few other instruments. One day Pops came to the Chaplain's office and told us that he needed prayer so that someone in his family would write to him. Pops had lost all contact with his family. We gathered around Pops and prayed over him in asking God to please help in reconnecting Pops with his family members who lived back east somewhere.

About two are three weeks later one of Pop's cousins in Florida found Pops online and wrote him a letter. This led to pictures which led to a phone call and to Pops surprise his son now in his twenties who had not spoken to his father in years talked to his dad and at the end of the conversation told his father that he loved him...

The reason why I'm sharing this story with you is because no matter how much time as passed between having any contact between those we love do not give up hope because God is in full control. It's never too late to reach out to someone we love and say, I love you. (1 Corinthians Chapter 13)

Ken was a Christian Counselor who visited the prison regularly. Ken helped teach the Maximized Manhood curriculum. One night while Ken was teaching he asked those of us who were there if anyone was in need of prayer because of any health problems that they may be dealing with. A man with chronic back pain came forward in need of prayer. The man had no idea what was causing his pain. Ken asked the man to lay down on the floor and after doing so Ken noticed that one of the man's legs was about two inches shorter than the other. Ken invited the Body of Christ who were there that night to please come forward and pray over this man.

After a few minutes of prayer by the laying of hands of the Body of Christ the man's shorter leg grew two inches right before our eyes. The man's back pain was gone, he was healed for the glory of God and in so doing this miracle of God energized the Body of Christ at Kingman Prison.

This next story is about Greg, the gentle giant. Greg was a big guy and one of the nicest guys you could ever meet. Greg was married and had two small children at the time he was at Kingman. One day when Greg called home his wife told him that she had met another man and wanted a divorce. She told Greg that the other man had already moved in with her and the kids and that she never wanted to speak to Greg ever again. Greg came to the Chaplain's office in tears, it was heartbreaking, I felt so bad for my Brother in Christ.

We all gathered around Greg and prayed for God's mercy, guidance and love in this situation. Then to make matters worse, Greg had to have all of his teeth pulled. That's the way bad teeth are dealt with in prison. I prayed with Greg every day. I tried to cheer him up and to give him hope. I prayed that Greg's wife would have a change of heart and for all of this mess to somehow work itself out in a good way for Greg.

Soon after, Greg came walking in the Chapel with a big toothless smile on his face and told us that his wife had a change of heart and that she kicked the other guy out of the house. She told Greg that she loves him and that she was very sorry. Even now ten years later I will say it again,

Thank You, Thank You, Thank You Abba Father for all of your blessings and love in helping to restore Greg's marriage.

Here is the story about my friend John who was cured of Hep-C by the power of prayer and by laying of hands by the Body of Christ at Kingman.

John was a really nice guy like Greg. John suffered from Hep-C, he had gotten the disease a few years back after getting a tattoo. Just a side note, he did not get his tattoo in prison. After he was diagnosed with having Hep-C John freaked out and started shooting up meth. John soon found himself locked up in jail then eventually he was sent to prison at Kingman.

One night as John and I were walking around the track on the south yard, we heard a group of guys singing and praising the Lord in Spanish so we walked over to check it out. They were ten Christian dudes from Mexico singing, clapping their hands and praising God. John and I introduced ourselves and then we told them about John's illness. Well, these guys made a prayer circle around John and told John to sit on the ground in the center of the prayer circle.

Then these mighty Brothers in Christ began praying their hearts out to the lord for John to be healed. I was praying with them in the prayer circle as well. When I tell you that these guys were praying their hearts out I mean it. Some of these guys were crying real tears. They were begging for God's divine mercy in healing John of his Hep-C. After this experience I'll say this, when it's my turn to have to deal with major health problems, I'm seeking out my Brothers and Sisters in Christ who are Spanish to pray over me.

Chaplain Lewis and the Body of Christ at the Chapel also prayed over John after this incident out on the yard. First let me explain about having Hep-

C in prison. The only thing that the doctors and nurses can do at medical is monitor your enzymes in your liver and when the level reaches a certain point you get sent off to a real hospital for treatment.

About a week later John went to medical for his usual enzyme check and to the Doctor's shocking surprise John's liver was in full remission, it had reversed itself and was now repairing itself for the glory of God. That had only happened three other times in the history of Kingman State Prison where a person's liver with Hep-C was in full remission and now repairing itself. One of the other two inmates who was healed was Brother Chooie who not only was cured of his Hep-C but was also cured of his diabetes as well by the power of prayer and by the laying of hands by Chaplain Lewis and the Body of Christ at Kingman. One of the other inmates who was cured was Brother Robert who was my Assistant Pod Pastor and right hand man in ministry on the South Yard. Robert was also cured of his Hep-C by the power of prayer and by the laying of hands of the body of Christ. I have no doubt that the fourth inmate who was healed of this disease was also a believer in Christ Yeshua at Kingman State Prison.

Willy was an older African American man who was serving time at Kingman. Willy was almost completely blind. Each day this poor man would walk around the prison crying because he could not see. Now, I do not mean to say he was complaining,

I mean he was sobbing quietly to himself as he walked around the yard. Then one night as my Brothers in Christ were closing out the north yard in a prayer circle, Willy walked over to join them. My Brothers in Christ prayed over Willy in asking for God's mercy and healing. Then like a flash of light Willy's eyes were opened and he could see once again. When the body of Christ at Kingman were told of this miracle of God we all became energized because of God's infinite power and love.

Mark 10:46-52

Blind Bartimaeus Receives His Sight

46 Then they came to Jericho. As Jesus and his disciples, together with a large crowd, were leaving the city, a blind man, Bartimaeus (which means "son of Timaeus"), was sitting by the roadside begging.

47 When he heard that it was Jesus of Nazareth, he began to shout, "Jesus, Son of David, have mercy on me!"

48 Many rebuked him and told him to be quiet, but he shouted all the more, "Son of David, have mercy on me!"

49 Jesus stopped and said, "Call him."

So they called to the blind man, "Cheer up! On your feet! He's calling you."

50 Throwing his cloak aside, he jumped to his feet and came to Jesus.

51 "What do you want me to do for you?" Jesus asked him.

The blind man said, "Rabbi, I want to see."

52 "Go," said Jesus, "your faith has healed you." Immediately he received his sight and followed Jesus along the road.

James 5:13-16 Faith Prays for the Afflicted

Is anyone among you suffering? Let him pray. Is anyone cheerful? Let him sing psalms. Is anyone among you sick? Let him call for the elders of the Church, and let them pray over him, anointing him with oil in the Name of the Lord. And the prayer of faith will save the sick and the Lord will raise him up. And if he has committed sins, he will be forgiven. Confess your trespasses to one another, and pray for one another, that you may be healed. The effective, fervent prayer of a righteous man avails much...Amen

Chapter Seven
And The Walls Come
Tumbling Down

One day as I was sitting in the Chaplain's office Billy knocked on the door and asked to see Chaplain Basye. I was sitting by the door so I could open it for people who wanted to see the Chaplain.

Billy was born again but like the rest of us he hadn't always been that way in his past. Billy was involved in a whole slew of criminal activities before he gave his life to Christ. Billy had been in and out of jail many times over the years. Billy had a younger brother who he was at odds with. The brothers no longer talked to each other, and to top it off his mother was very upset with Billy. Billy had come to see Chaplain Basye because he had been diagnosed with cancer and wanted to call his mother and make peace with her and his younger brother. Chaplain Basye allowed Billy to make a phone call. There were only three of us in the office at the time. Billy called his mother and she informed him that his younger brother was killed in a truck accident just two weeks prior. Billy's mother also told him that she didn't want anything to do with him, then she hung up on him. Billy was heartbroken, then a very interesting thing happened; Chaplain Basye got up and walked around from behind his desk and sat down right in front of Billy. I have to say the way Chaplain Basye stood up from behind his desk and the way he walked around with a look of total concern on his face, then pulled up a chair and sat down right in front of Billy reminded me of John F. Kennedy.

Chaplain Basye then said this prayer as if Christ was sitting right next to them, and He was.

"Lord as a personal favor to me please restore Billy's relationship with his mother."

I have to tell you, I started to cry, the whole thing was very sad. Billy was crying, I got up and walked over to Billy and placed my hand on his shoulder then Chaplain Basye prayed over Billy.

Afterword Billy simply got up, thanked us and walked back to his pod. The very next day was Wednesday and on Wednesday night is Intercessory Prayer night at the Chapel. Every Wednesday we as the Body of Christ at Kingman Prison gather up all the prayer requests that were placed in the prayer boxes in every pod in the prison. Then we place all the prayer requests on a table in the Chapel and form a prayer circle around the table and say a prayer. Each of us takes four or five prayer requests and go pray on our knees for the needs of others. The service lasts about an hour then we close out the service in prayer. On this night as I was praying by the door I noticed from the corner of my eye that Chaplain Basye and his wife Sandy had walked in. This was strange because Chaplain Basye had already gone home for the day. He usually leaves the prison at around three pm. on Wednesdays, so seeing both him and Sandy walk through the door was concerning. I stood up and walked over to the Chaplain and asked him if everything was alright. He looked shaken, and by the look on his face I honestly thought that someone had died.

Before we close out the service we set chairs in a circle around the table with the prayer requests. We all sit and take turns talking about what the Lord is doing in each of our lives, it reminded me like we were Jedi Knights for the Lord. After each of us is given a chance to speak we stand up and then pray out the service. When we stood up Chaplain Basye told us that he had something that he wanted to share with all of us.

Chaplain Basye said that Billy's mother had been calling all around the state trying to reach him all day and finally got a hold of him on his cell phone as he was driving down the highway and said,

"I'm sorry Chaplain, I don't know what came over me, I love my son and I want him in my life,"

Chaplain Basye was so moved by what had taken place that he felt compelled to come back to the prison that same night and tell Billy personally in front of the Body of Christ.

After we all heard the news we all began hugging Billy and praising God because Chaplain Basye's personal prayer to God was answered.

Afterward, we all gathered together in a big prayer circle and then I looked at everyone and said,

"Brothers in the book of acts Paul and Silas were chained to a wall in the prison at midnight, first they prayed then they sang, then the walls of the prison came tumbling down." (As in their chains unlocked and fell to the floor and the doors to the prison were suddenly opened setting Paul and Salas free)

I looked at my Brothers in Christ who were there that faithful night and repeated myself,

"Brothers, first we are going to pray then we are going to sing praises to the Lord then the walls of this prison are going to come tumbling down."

First we prayed, then we sang, and I will tell you it felt like God poured a bucket of joy on all of our heads that night. We first sang in English then in Spanish, it was awesome, we prayed and sang our hearts out that faithful night in giving our Lord thanks and praise.

Then just as we finished a young inmate walked through the door and asked to see Chaplain Basye. I folded up the table and right when I placed it on top of the other folded tables the whole prison went black. There was a total blackout of the prison. Chaplain Basye, Sandy and the inmate were in the dark in his office. Then the prison generators kicked on and the lights came back on and the loudspeakers told all inmates to return to our pods.

As we were all running back to our pods we were all praising God. God did exactly as I said. First we prayed then we sang then the walls of the prison came tumbling down for the glory of God. Now please let me explain all of this to you. The prison walls that came tumbling down that night were the walls that satan had built up between Billy and his Mother. The blackout was confirmation of God's infinite power and love in this situation and that He is in full control of all things. He was there with all of us that night. He was there with Chaplain Basye, Billy and myself. He is there with you right now and He is sitting right here with me as I write these stories for this book so that one day He will be glorified by it...Amen

Acts Chapter 16: 25-34

25 About midnight Paul and Silas were praying and singing hymns to God, and the prisoners were listening to them, 26 and suddenly there was a great earthquake, so that the foundations of the prison were shaken. And immediately all the doors were opened, and everyone's bonds were unfastened. 27 When the jailer woke and saw that the prison doors were open, he drew his sword and was about to kill himself, supposing that the prisoners had escaped. 28 But Paul cried with a loud voice, "Do not harm yourself, for we are all here." 29 And the jailer called for lights and rushed in, and trembling with fear he fell down before Paul and Silas. 30 Then he brought them out and said, "Sirs, what must I do to

be saved?" 31 And they said, "Believe in the Lord Yeshua, and you will be saved, you and your household." 32 And they spoke the word of the Lord to him and to all who were in his house. 33 And he took them the same hour of the night and washed their wounds; and he was baptized at once, he and all his family. 34 Then he brought them up into his house and set food before them. And he rejoiced along with his entire household that he had believed in God.

Chapter Eight
Prayer Boxes n Prayer Circles

As I sit at my desk and begin to write this next chapter I paused and looked over at the prayer box that now sits on my desk. The prayer box that's sitting on my desk is very special to me because it was the first one that Gabriel made for me. Gabriel is my brother in Christ and he was a very good friend of mine while I was in Kingman. Gabriel handcrafted beautiful hand made prayer boxes using very simple materials. Each prayer box was made out of a cracker box that was shortened in height then white paper was glued onto the front and back and on the sides, then Gabriel painted beautiful pictures on the back of the prayer box. Each prayer box was framed by crafting Popsicle sticks that were painted in a variety of colors. He also added a small cross to the top of each prayer box.

This next story is about a guy named Steve and his faith in God in putting a prayer request in my prayer box each day.

Steve De was Italian like I am and we got along very well. Steve was always making jokes about his situation and he made me laugh each time he told one. Steve was serving time for a D.U.I. He was

MIRACLES OF KINGMAN STATE PRISON

sentenced to five years for his crimes. When an inmate has served at least half their time they can put in a request for an arbitration hearing. Steve's lawyer had really dropped the ball in Steve's case. There were many incompetent mistakes made by Steve's attorney, and those mistakes cost Steve dearly. Steve told me that his arbitration hearing was coming up soon and that he was very worried about it. I recommended to Steve that he write out a prayer request and put it in the box each day and that he also come to me for prayer. He agreed and praying with Steve each day really helped in calming him down about having to go to court. When an inmate has to go to court it's not like it is on the outside. The inmate is rolled up and shipped to a Phoenix jail to await trial, it can really suck if things get delayed.

This was the main reason why I was freaking out about having to deal with the courts concerning my son while in prison. I totally sympathized with Steve's concerns about this issue.

Meanwhile, as this was going on with Steve another friend of mine who's name we will call Big Jim was researching the origins of the name Jesus. Jim was a very serious inmate the kind of guy you do not want to piss off. The good news was Jim is Christian and we got along fine. Jim was on a very strict walk with the lord and Jim was highly studied in the word. Unfortunately, Jim would push his walk on baby Christians and confuse their walk with Christ. Here let me explain, let's say the Holy Spirit places it on your heart to be a vegetarian to teach you something or to improve your health. You are not to go running around telling other Christians that they are not good Christians if they're not vegetarian. Do you see what I'm getting at here? In some cases in our walk with Christ just because God tells you to do something, it doesn't always mean that everyone else has got to do the exact same thing that you are being told to do.

Then one day as I was standing out in the south yard with Bobby my Brother in Christ, along comes Big Jim and begins blaspheming the name Jesus because there is no J in the Hebrew alphabet. I personally dug into this same subject for years and I'm not going to get into it here.

Truthfully I did not know what Big Jim was talking about and he got extremely agitated that day. At some point, Bobby looked at him and said.

"I remove the dust of my shoes of you."

Then Bobby walked back to our pod. So there I was standing out on the South Yard trying to calm Big Jim down. Finally, I was able to calm him down a little. Then the yard closed down for count just before lunch and we both walked back to our pods. I honestly could not understand where Big Jim was coming from but I do now and still I would never blaspheme the name of Jesus like he did that day.

Later as I was in the chow hall eating lunch my heads came up to me asking what I had said to Jim. They thought we were fighting when we were talking out on the yard. I told them that we were just talking and that Big Jim sometimes gets loud and a little carried away about things, which they knew very well about Jim. My heads told me that Big Jim had gotten rolled up. Upon hearing this I began to get very concerned because if the heads thought that I had anything to do with Big Jim getting rolled up I could get hurt and get hurt very badly.

I found out later that same day that Big Jim was rolled up because he refused to tie his hair up over at medical. Big Jim had long white hair and the rule was that when you walk off of the yard you have to tie your hair in a ponytail. Big Jim made a fuss and was taken to the lieutenant and then he pissed the lieutenant off and the lieutenant ordered Big Jim rolled up and placed in the hole and moved to another prison. The hole is a single holding cell.

Then about three days later, here comes Steve De with the biggest smile you ever saw. Steve's arbitration hearing went very well for him, not only was Steve's time cut in half, but with his 1291 early kick out Steve was now going home in less than thirty days. Steve's time went from having to face two and a half more years to now less than thirty days for the glory of God...

Now here's the lesson in all of this. There are over fifteen hundred inmates at Kingman and there were at least seventy or more available open beds at any given time. When an inmate has to go to court they lose their space and are issued a new one when they return to the prison.

Upon Steve's return he was issued a new bed. Now, remember he has got roughly about a hundred to one shot of receiving a certain bed. Steve's new assigned space was Big Jim's old spot. One person was obedient to God each day and was blessed with less time, peace and great joy. The other person was disobedient to God for blaspheming the Lord's name and was rolled up and punished right on the spot. I have to say when I found out what really happened that faithful day I was shocked, especially after finding out that Steve De was placed in Big Jim's old space. that's called confirmation by Abba Father without a shadow of a doubt...Amen

Donovan was serving as Head Pastor of the south yard, I served under him as a Pod Pastor and in the time we shared together at Kingman Donovan taught me a lot about being a Christian. Then one day, he too was sent off on a shift change. The following Wednesday night after Donovan's departure as I was standing in a prayer circle with my Bothers in Christ during Intercessory Prayer Service, Brother Nacho who was the Head Chaplain's Clerk said something to me that caught me off guard. I didn't hear what he said so I looked over at him and said,

"What do you say Brother Nacho?"

"The Holy Spirit has elected you as the new Head Pastor of the south yard."

Believe it or not, that honor means more to me than graduating as a Chaplain. Being appointed by the Body of Christ through the leadings of the Holy Spirit to be the Head Pastor of the South Yard was and still is one of the greatest honors of my life. I took the responsibility very seriously. I soon organized the building of prayer boxes for every pod in the prison. Doug, Tracy whom I called Brother Hugs, and Robert and I encouraged the Body of Christ at Kingman to create medicine chests and hygiene chests on each yard. Robert and I streamlined the tithing procedure for the Church. I had a beautiful hand made cross made for the pulpit.

I had also asked Chaplain Basye if he could help in getting Bibles and devotionals in the holding cells over at medical. That deal took over a year of persuading with the prison authority. I would ask the Chaplain about this issue from time to time and he would make a call only to be turned down by the staff over at medical.

I asked the Chaplain once again about getting Bibles and other Christian materials over at medical. He looked at me and said that he admired my perseverance concerning this matter. Once again he picked up the phone and placed a call to medical but instead of getting turned down, this time the staff member transferred him over to a medical supervisor and when she heard about what we wanted to do she loved the idea and approved it. After the call Chaplain Basye gave me a reassuring look and then gave me the honor of bringing Bibles and devotional's over to medical to be placed in the holding cells for inmates. Inmates who got sick at night were forced to sleep in those cells and suffer until medical staff arrived the next day. Now at least they will have something good to read to pass the time.

Here's a short story about a guy named Slim. Slim looked like the typical tall thin cowboy that we see in the old time TV shows and movies. Slim was a nice guy. Slim had come to see the Chaplain to ask for prayer because he had no money on his books. When an inmate has no family support they basically starve and do without. Oh sure you can get food over at chow three times a day but not having any store at your space is very rough. That's where the Body of Christ comes in by helping someone like Slim. We gave of our food, medicine, and even clothing at times in helping other inmates. The Body Of Christ at Kingman helped inmates write letters to receive Bibles, we also helped in writing letters to the courts on occasion.

At Kingman State Prison the Body of Christ was more than just inmates who wanted to get back home, we were and still are the light of Christ to the world. Kingman was like a Bible Boot Camp that trained up men for ministry work around the world. We were like seeds on a dandelion when the wind blows. The Holy Spirit touches our lives and just like the seeds of a dandelion we take to the air and when we finally touch down on futile soil we begin to grow and bear fruit for the glory of God.

Well after we prayed over Slim in asking God to please help in receiving some badly needed money he went back to his pod and there laying on his bunk was a letter and when he opened and read it, he was shocked to learn that a friend of his had placed some money on his books. Coincidence? I don't think so, its all in the timing when it comes to the miracles and blessings of God.

Prayer circles are a very powerful way to pray to God. Every night the Body of Christ at Kingman would go out on each of the three yards and form a prayer circle to close out the yard. Each person in the prayer circle was given a chance to pray, then when everyone had prayed individually everyone prays in unison and when we're finished we all shout,

"WHAT'S HIS NAME? JESUS!!! WHAT'S HIS NAME? JESUS!!!WHAT'S HIS NAME? JESUS!!!!!!!"

And because all three yards closed out at the same time each night we could hear each other's shout out from the other two yards. It was very cool, it made me feel like we were all family, and re-alistically that is exactly how the Body of Christ is meant to be.

Each year on the first Thursday of May is the National Day of Prayer. This year Chaplain Basye had a great idea he wanted each yard to organize a giant prayer circle by inviting anyone who wanted to attend on each yard. Our prayer circles were open to everyone each night but the prayer circles on the National Day of Prayer would be promoted in-advance by spreading the word throughout the prison in inviting as many inmates as we could to attend on that special day of prayer.

Well, the powers the be got wind of it and told Chaplain Basye to shut the idea down because they felt it could insight a riot. Their concerns were that having all races coming together and holding hands in a prayer circle might make the other inmates up-set and start fighting over the issue. You see in prison the different races are not allowed to share unwrapped food with each other and they're not al-lowed to touch each other. These rules were not prison rules as handed down by the D.O.C. Depart-ment Of Corrections. These rules were handed down by the heads of each individual race.

So the Warden shut down our prayer circles and would not allow the Chaplains to organize the event. Then we as the Body of Christ decided to go ahead and organize it ourselves and that is exactly what we did. Tough bananas D.O.C.

On the morning of the National Day of Prayer, I stepped out onto the South Yard in faith. I did not know how many inmates would show up that day. The plan was, certain pod Pastors on my yard would pray in the circle, I would pray last, then all three yards would shout out,

"WHAT'S HIS NAME? JESUS!!! WHAT'S HIS NAME? JESUS!!! WHAT'S HIS NAME? JESUS!!!!!!!"

So there I was standing all by myself waiting to

see who would show and here comes my Head Mr. Tucker walking by and says.

"I don't think anyone is going to show up for your little prayer circle there."

"Well, you are more than welcome to come join us Mr. Tucker."

"No, that's Ok, I'll pass on it this time."

"Have a blessed day Sir."

Then one by one inmates began to arrive, soon there were over eighty inmates in our circle on the South Yard. We all joined hands, then one by one each Pod Pastor in our prayer circle prayed. When it was time for me to pray I looked up to the heavens and began to pray my heart out to Abba Father for our families, for the inmates, for the staff and for the Body of Christ at Kingman. I have to tell you God filled me with great peace, love and joy that day and when I was finished we did our What's His Name Jesus shout out in perfect timing with the North Yard, the East Yard did their shout out a few minutes later.

A short time later the Deputy Warden told Chaplain Basey that in over thirty years working for D.O.C. (Department Of Corrections) he had never seen anything like that where all races came together holding hands in prayer.

Please try forming a prayer circle of your own with your family. Family prayer circles are very powerful in casting out the powers of darkness in our lives, and family prayer circles help in strengthening family harmony, unity, peace, love, and joy...Amen Psalms 91

Before I end this chapter I just want to tell you about Chaplain Lewis. Chaplain Lewis was an old school southern Christian. He looked and acted like a Drill Sergeant for the Lord. He was a seventy year old short stocky man with a bald head and he is a mighty man of God. Many inmates were healed at Kingman while I was there by the laying of hands and prayer by Chaplain Lewis and the Body of Christ. Chaplain Lewis would begin his Bible Study and other Church services with this shout,

"Now men please repeat after me, JESUS I LOVE YOU, HOLY SPIRIT I LOVE YOU, FATHER GOD I LOVE YOU, THIS IS THE DAY THAT THE LORD HAS MADE, I WILL REJOICE AND BE GLAD IN IT, BECAUSE I WALK BY FAITH AND NOT BY SIGHT, FAITH COMES BY HEARING AND HEARING COMES BY THE WORD OF THE LORD. HOLY SPIRIT TAKE CHARGE OF MY LIFE, GUIDE ME, MOLD ME, AND SHAPE ME INTO THE LIKENESS OF CHRIST JESUS, I LOVE YOU AND I PRAISE YOU IN JESUS HOLY NAME WE PRAY...AMEN!!!!!!!"

Now imagine over fifty inmates of the Body of Christ all standing at attention shouting that out each day.

Remember, I said that Kingman was like a Bible Boot Camp for all those who were in the Body of

Christ at that time. Well Ole Chaplain Lewis was a one of a kind Bible Boot Camp Drill Sergeant for sure. Chaplain Lewis would not tolerate any complaining or crybaby stuff from members of the Body of Christ. He would always say,

"Don't let yourselves get pulled down into the molligrubs,

NOW MEN, I DO NOT WANT TO HEAR ANY MOLLIGRUBING COMING FROM YOU ALL. NOW MEN, STAND UP FOR THE LORD AND BE STRONG MEN OF GOD FOR HIS GLORY AMEN!!!

My Blessings

Chapter Nine
Christmas at Kingman

Christmas-Eve 2008 was my first Christmas in Prison, and on that very special night at Church, Chaplain Basye offered Communion to all of us who were in attendance. Chaplain Basye explained that when we receive Communion we enter into a deeper relationship with Christ. As we enter into Communion with Christ we remember all of the things that He has done for us throughout our lives, then we remember Him dying on the cross so that our sins could be forgiven. My Brothers in Christ who were there that faithful night stood in line and then one by one received Communion. We all went back to our seats, some of us got on our knees in prayer, and others bent over in prayer as they sat in their seats. As we prayed in silence many of us began to weep. The Spirit of God had filled the room with Christ's love that faithful night. There was beautiful music playing in the background as the service unfolded. I have to say, even now ten years later, that Communion Service at Kingman State Prison on Christmas-Eve night was the most moving Communion Service that I have ever attended in my life. Matthew 26:26-29. Sometimes God would place very difficult people in my life during my stay at Kingman. I called these people my assignments. Warren was one of my assignments. Warren was a very negative person most of the time, I did manage to get along with him through my faith in Christ. Warren would go on to play a key role and a key part in the Christmas play that we put on at the prison. Another one of my assignments was a guy by the name of Jonathan. Jonathan was a very troubled young man and what eventually happened to Jonathan serves as a warning to us all not to interfere with Abba Father's anointed people, places or things. I'll tell you more about Warren and Jonathan later in this chapter.

Anthony was another one of my assignments at Kingman. Anthony was a young kid in his twenties who could not read or write very well but at the same time was a very talented artist. Anthony was the kind of person who liked to get in people's space. Anthony was very intrusive with the other inmates and he got into fights all the time. If you were talking to Anthony he would say things like,

"Oh, I know that." or "I knew that."

This was to cover up his insecurity of not being able to read or write very well.

One day as we were walking over by the mail room Anthony started getting handsy with me. Like poking at me for fun. Well first of all I do not like being touched like that, I'm not a horsing around kinda guy. Anthony pulled this kinda stuff with me before and I put him in his place, but this time it got more out of hand and I yelled at him and he walked away. At that point Abba Father said to me in my spirit,

Anthony is a representation of your son and you are to treat that boy with love and kindness."

I get it God, Anthony was of Italian descent and he did not know who his father was. Get the picture here. God may have sent me a rainbow but He didn't let me off the hook in having to deal with the heartbreak concerning my son. I began teaching Anthony about the Bible, we would have talks in the pod. Anthony was two beds away from me in the same row of the pod. In time Anthony would watch over me like Jimmy and my friend John were doing. I encouraged Anthony to create beautiful birthday and Christmas cards for my family. I paid him with store products for his labor. I still have some of his cards to this day.

In October of 2009, God gave me a vision for the prison. I walked over to the Chapel to see Chaplain Basye to tell him about it. I asked the Chaplain if we could put on a Christian Christmas play at the prison called Scrooge a Christmas Carol. The Chaplain asked the Warden and she loved the idea. Then Chaplain Basye said,

"Write the script, but remember Paul, we have to be as wise as serpents and as gentle as doves in creating this play, we can't be to Christian in your face about this, we need to play it real cool."

I went back to my pod and began writing the

script that same day. I was writing so fast that I had to have my Assistant Pod Pastor Robert rewrite what I had written so that it was more legible to the reader. I was now not only the Head Pastor of the South Yard, but was also the Writer and the Director of a Christmas Play with a small singing part towards the end of the production.

I made a list of characters that were needed for the play. I wrote the script Christian based with what I had remembered seeing in the movie Scrooge a Christmas Carol with Albert Finney back in the 70s. I watched this same movie every Christmas Eve for years, so I knew how to merge what I had in memory with my imagination with the Holy Spirit's help for the glory of God.

Then I went around the prison with a clipboard and pencil and hand - picked all the actors needed to fill all the parts in the play. God set the whole thing up perfectly the inmates matched the actor's in the movie that I had remembered seeing, it was unbelievable.

Tiny Tim was this small little guy named David, Scrooge was played by Doug my Brother in Christ. Doug was tall and he had long white hair he looked and played the role of Scrooge perfectly. Robert my Assistant Pod Pastor was the Assistant Director and Narrator. Jacob Marley was played by Billy and he did an excellent job. Bob Cratchit was played by a guy named Walter who looked just like Bob Cratchit in the movies. I used the names of the prophets in the Bible for the merchants in the play, like Mr. Isaiah was a Bible Salesman and Mr. Jeremiah sold Daily Bread Devotionals and Mr Ezekiel sold scarves and socks with Mr. Habakkuk being a soup vendor who was played by David and who was extremely funny at it. I wrote in a Puppet Master and two brothers who sold tamales. A guy by the name of Blue who I will tell you more about later in this book played a Christmas ghost. The play had humor and music and packed a very powerful message for the glory of God. Chaplain Basye played the part of old Fuzzy Winkel and sang a song called, This Is The Day That The Lord Has Made. His wife Sandy played the only women's part in the play because of prison rules. Sandy played the role of Ruth who was Scrooge's wife in Christmas Past.

There were over fifty inmates who signed on for this production all voluntary with very little supervision. Brother Israel was my musical director. Brother Israel was a seasoned musician who wrote his own music and played a number of instruments. Israel played the keyboard for the production and directed all the music for the play.

As the production began to get underway with rehearsals, two and three times a week, some inmates quit, while still others were rolled up and shipped out to other prisons, and still others got sick by showtime. I had to have all of my bases covered. I had understudies on standby just in case something happened to key actors. I began to assign titles for key production possessions that were needed to make all of this work... I created titles and acting roles so as to give inmates purpose and a sense of self worth. Remember Warren, Jonathan and Anthony? I gave each of them a title with certain specific responsibilities in helping to create this play. Warren was my Prop Director and played the role of the Spirit of Christmas Future. Remember Pops? Pops was our Understudy and played the Spirit of Christmas Present because Fred who was to play the role was sent to the hole. Brother Curtis played the role of the Spirit of Christmas Past. Brother Love who was a man who was filled with the love of Christ was the play's official Greeter. Anthony was placed in charge of making all the decorations that decorated the Chapel for the production. Oh, and Jonathan was given the title of Stage Crew Foreman. Warren was very upset about that because he said it wasn't unnecessary, but after I explained to him the importance of building up Jonathan's self esteem and giving him a sense of self worth he finally agreed and left the issue alone.

When rehearsals first began I thought that the play was going to be this cheesy production with no costumes, boy was I wrong about that. I soon learned that when God places a vision on a person's heart He pulls out all the stops in seeing it through for His glory. Soon the Basyes would start bringing in makeshift costumes and arts and crafts to make props and decorations for the play. Kingman Prison had a building trades department where children's playhouses and other handcrafted wooden items were made for auction for charity events. We had expert wood craters, skilled painters and seasoned artists all helping to build the necessary props and scenery for the play. We had a city scene, a cemetery scene, a fireplace scene, we had a coffin and hand-crafted furniture built for the play. We even had a Christmas tree. I have to say, this production was an amazing thing to watch grow.

Warren was key in organizing the props and the timing of when certain props needed to be changed throughout the production of the play. Then one day Warren came to me and said that Jonathan was trying to sabotage God's anointed play. I didn't believe Warren because I knew that he really did not like Jonathan, so I shrugged it off as being Warren's negativity once again. Warren kept telling me the same thing about Jonathan for about three days or so then he proved it to me by having me stand around the corner out of Jonathan's sight. Then I heard Jonathan telling lies about God's anointed play and got right in his face and set him straight big time.

I didn't kick him out of the play, I gave him a second chance after he apologized for what he had said. Here's a warning to all of us, do not mess with God, especially when something has been ordained by Him like the vision of His anointed play at Kingman State Prison. Here's what happened to Jonathan for his disobedience towards God. About two or three weeks before the presentation of the play while Jonathan was working with the skill saw in building trades, he sliced his hand right up the middle in between his ring finger and his middle finger. He was rushed to the hospital stitched up and then had to wear a cast on his hand and arm for about a month. Jonathan was still able to help with putting on the play, cast and all.

Everyone in the Body of Christ at Kingman put the word out for the play, we had fliers and announcements at all Church services and activities.

We all could not imagine how big of a turnout it would be. The Warden decided to allow two shows the first for inmates, and the second show for staff, inmate classes, and for state officials who came up just to see our little play.

The first show went perfectly, the second show the next day had some minor glitches, like the coffin was brought out to soon and Billy who played Jacob Marley skipped some of his lines but the audience didn't seem to notice.

Five hundred inmates come out to see our play for the glory of God. There were so many inmates who wanted to see it that they had to be turned away because they couldn't all fit in the Chapel. At the end of the play Scrooge gives his life to Christ and as he falls into the grave, we played the song Help by the Beatles, then has Scrooge awakens on Christmas Day as a new creation in Christ Jesus we played the song All You Need Is Love by the Beatles and as this song was being played, the Body of Christ started passing out candy-canes that the

Basyes had brought into the prison for the play. Each inmate received a hug and a candy-cane from a member of the Body of Christ at Kingman that faithful day.

Oh I almost forgot, I sang a song in the play called, Thank You Very Much. That was when Scrooge was in Christmas Future standing at his own funeral and did not know it as all the people were singing this song thanking him for dying so that all of their debts could be forgiven....Mmm-mmm now that sounds a little familiar...John 3:16 the only difference is we praise and love God for Christ's sacrifice in dying on the cross so that our sin debt could be forgiven... And with that,

"Thank You Very Much, Thank You Very Much, it's the nicest thing that anyone's ever done for me. I really am surprised, You've opened up my eyes, and now I'm a new creation in You O Lord..." Not bad wouldn't you say?

At the end of the play everyone, audience in-cluded sang Silent Night. I have no doubt that many inmates would eventually except Christ into their lives because of the spiritual seeds of faith that were planted in their hearts through Abba Fa-ther's anointed play. Then Chaplain Basye stepped forward and said,

"Paul, come up here, this is Paul Vescio, it was his vision that started this whole production. One person can make a big difference in a positive way in this world when they place their faith, hope and love in Christ our Lord. No other event brought out so many inmates for the glory of God then our little play here."

Then one by one, staff members and State Officials began walking up to me saying,

"Great job Mr. Vescio, you did a really good job putting this together."

Thank You Abba Father for helping to bring this awesome Christmas Play into the light of day for Your Glory. I give all the Praise, Glory, and Honor to You for helping in seeing it through.

Here are a few more Christmas goodies to add to this amazing story.

Before I continue with this Christmas story, since I mentioned hugging the inmates at our play, here is a story about another time when the Body of Christ at Kingman gave a kid by the name Brandon a huge hug. There was an Inmate who I met by the name of Brandon, Brandon was in his early twenties and was sent to prison for D.U.I.. Brandon was in the army in Iraq and was married, Brandon's baby son died and on the day of his sentencing, Brandon's wife was speeding to get to the hearing on time and was killed in a head on collision. Chaplain Basye asked if Brandon would please share his heartbreaking story with the Body of Christ. On the night that Brandon shared his story he also added that he had just been informed just a few days earlier that his father had been diagnosed with cancer. After Brandon shared his tragic story every inmate at the service that night stood in line and one by one gave Brandon a hug. There were about a hundred inmates there that night. No matter how bad we may think we have it in life there are always people out there who are going through far worse.

The day after the play was Christmas Eve and that night Chaplain Basye invited a Christian Cantata to come and perform at the prison. The singers in the Cantata were all dressed like you would see in a Norman Rockwell Magazine back in the day. They all sang beautifully. A Christian Cantata is where the performers sing songs based on the Bible and for that reason I think that's how Chaplain Basye was able to pull off having them come up to the prison to perform for all of us.

Then just when I thought it couldn't get any better for Christmas that year, Chaplain Basye and Sandy brought in over fourteen hundred Christmas cards for the inmates, all colored and signed by grade school children.

The body of Christ prayed over the cards asking God to please match the names on the cards to the inmate's family members. Soon an amazing thing began happening, inmates were receiving Christmas cards with their family member's names. Tino was Native American who had a daughter with a very unique name whom he hadn't seen for some time. The card that Tino opened had his daughter's name written in it. Tino was a true believer in Christ and one of my very good friends at the time.

I was asked to please take some of the cards back to my pod to hand out to the guys. I grabbed a stack of about twenty cards then I walked over to a table to open one for myself, as I opened the card and read the name on the Christmas card I was floored the name on the card was the same name as my girlfriend's. It didn't just happen to someone else, it actually happened to me and I still have that same Christmas card in my possession to this day.

On Christmas Day there was a special Church Service with Pastor Dee and then a special dinner was served at chow I forgot if it was ham or turkey. Then about ten days later on January 4 2010 on the exact same day of the fourteenth anniversary of my Father's death in 1996, I was released to come home. My family kept the Christmas tree up so that we could all spend Christmas together as a family. I have to tell you, that Christmas is in the top three all time greatest Christmases of my life, and we had some really great Christmases in my family over the years. And to think it happened in a prison, who knew? The true Directors of our lives knew.

This is what was written on the program for the play,

Director of Creation;	Father God
Spiritual Director;	The Holy Spirit
Director of Our Hearts;	Jesus Christ

Right before I was going to send this book off for publishing Abba Father placed on my heart to share with you the story of Blue. Blue was a young man who's whole face was tattooed, and because of this he developed some serious health problems. The tattoo turned his face blue, and people were afraid of him and rejected him. I will admit, at first glance I was very leary of approaching Blue. As time went on I began talking to Blue and soon realized that Blue had a heart of gold. Blue was a very kind and compassionate person. God had placed Blue in my life to teach me a very powerful lesson. All to often we may judge a book by its cover and not by its contents. People, myself included have excepted or rejected others based on their personal appearance and not by what was truly in their heart.

Blue was a perfect example of this truth., Before we judge a book we had better first take the time to thoroughly examine the contents of its pages. I have to admit, when I first saw Blue I was a little scared, because to be perfectly honest with you, he looked scary. Blue became one of my assignments and he played a ghost of the past in the Christmas Play.

The lesson we can all learn from my friend and Brother in Christ Blue is;

when we come in contact with the homeless, or when we come in contact with someone who is transgender or disabled, handicapped or of a different race, religion or culture, or even an ex-offender, we need to first get to know what's in their heart before we decide to except or reject them. Always remember, it's what's in a person's heart that truly matters...Amen

First Samuel 16:7 But the Lord said to Samuel, "Do not look at his appearance or at his physical stature, because I have refused him. For the Lord does not see as man sees: for man looks at the outward appearance, but the Lord looks at the heart.

My Blessings

Chapter Ten
One Person Plants Another Waters and God Provides the Increase

When Pastor Jose left the prison on a shift change, there was a slight problem. so I went to see Chaplain Basye about it.

"Chaplain, who is going to do the Bible Study now that Pastor Jose is gone?"

The Chaplain looked right at me and said,

"Paul, I want you to do it."

"Me? I don't know anything about leading a Bible study Chaplain."

"Paul, just read the word and talk about it, keep it simple."

Well that was it, I called home and asked my family to please send me the John MacArthur Study Bible. I asked God what book of the Bible to do the Bible study on. The message I get back was, do First Timothy. Back then I was a baby Christian and I didn't have a clue of what First Timothy was all about. When I received the Study Bible I dove right into the text, so much so I strained my eyes. I did not want to let Chaplain Basye down, I did not want to let the Body of Christ down and most of all I did not want to let Abba Father down. You have to understand this Bible study was very special because it was inmates only and it was all ours for the glory of God.

At first the Bible study got off to a rocky start, then an interesting thing happened, I realized that this Bible study really didn't belong to us, it belonged to the Holy Spirit. I soon realized that our little Bible study belonged to God. So I humbly gave it completely to Him. The way that I officiated the study was we would begin reading First Timothy and if at any point anyone felt a connection to the word as in the scripture verse aligned with their particular circumstances then raise your hand and you will be given a chance to share your thoughts with those in the Bible study.

Now I have to tell you, there were some of my Brothers in Christ who were very highly studied and who were upset that Chaplain Basye chose me to lead the inmate Bible Study. One of whom was Brother Adolph. Brother Adolph was highly studied in the word and he felt that it should have been him who was chosen to lead the study. I remember Brother Adolph coming to the study and asking those who were there what they wanted to study. It was very disheartening and troubling for me. Then one time he came to the study and sat right next to me and said,

"Let's study something else today, I brought something with me that we can all study."

I simply placed my hand on Brother Adolph's wrist and said,

"Brother Adolph, Chaplain Basye chose me to lead this Bible Study, if you have any problem with that then let's go see the Chaplain and discuss it with him."

After I said that, Brother Adolph stood up and walked out of the room.

I respected Brother Adolph greatly, he and so many other of my Brothers in Christ at Kingman were like mentors to me. They taught me a great many things about being a Christian while I was in Kingman.

I soon began to feel bad about what had happened, then a strange thing happened. God placed on my heart to go and apologize to Brother Adolph. I could not understand why, after all I did not do anything wrong but God was teaching me a very powerful lesson in forgiveness and in defeating satan.

I walked over to Brother Adolph's pod on the south yard and looked him in the eye and said,

"Brother Adolph, I am very sorry if I said or if I have done anything to hurt or offend you, that was not my intentions, I respect you and hope you will accept my apology."

Brother Adolph was stunned, he knew deep in his heart that he was treating me poorly and here I was apologizing to him. Brother Adolph was touched by the Spirit then he apologized to me and in so doing satan was defeated and the wall that he had tried to build between Brother Adolph and myself was broken and came tumbling down for the glory of God...

When a Bible Study is given to God in faith and love and the Holy Spirit is able to freely move in the midst of it then the blessings of peace, love and joy are poured out on to all those who are in attendance, like a fountain of living water for the glory of God.

Now, for me to finish up this chapter I have to first go all the way back to the beginning of this story. When Kingman State Prison first opened there was no Church of Kingman like I had experienced. There were no Christian programs or Pod Pastors or Bible Studies or Praise and Worship Band. All of those things had not yet been created. Chaplain Eddie was the first Chaplain at Kingman and when he first arrived at the prison he anointed all the prison cells and proclaimed Kingman State Prison as being Holy Ground for the glory of God. Just as a farmer prepares the soil for planting physically, Men and Women of God prepare the hearts of others along with places like the prison and our homes spiritually for the glory of God.

My friend Mike lived on the same block that I did in Scottsdale Arizona. Mike and I have been through thick and thin together. We were like brothers back in the day, there was a whole group of us who lived on the same two streets side by side, we all watched out for each other, we were and still are Pals for life. Mike died a few years ago due to alcohol abuse. Before I got sent to Kingman, Mike had gone to prison a few years prior on a drug charge. When Mike returned home he would always talk fondly about the Church at the prison where he was sent to. I never asked him which prison he was in.

Then in 2008, it was now my turn to go to prison and I wound up in Kingman. When I arrived there a mighty harvest was well underway for the glory of God. Little did I now that it was my friend Mike who helped in planting the seeds for that harvest.

Mike was hired as Kingman State Prison's first inmate Chaplain's Clerk.

Mike served under Chaplain Eddie. It was Mike along with the other members of the Body of Christ (which was very few at the time) who sat down together and prayed to God for His guidance and love in growing the Church of Kingman.

After I returned back home in 2010, about a three years later I reunited with Mike and at some point, I finally asked him what prison did he go to. When he told me Kingman I was shocked, then when he said that he was the first Chaplain's Clerk to be hired there, I was stunned. That means we are of the same Church and that Mike was my senior in the Body of Christ. Unbelievable.

As time went on we began sharing stories about our stay at Kingman, then one day as I was sitting talking to Mike, I asked him who led the inmate Bible Study at Kingman? Mike looked over at me and said, "He did." Then I said, "So did I." You have to understand in the history of that prison only a hand full of inmates of the Body of Christ led that Bible Study. I would place the number at around five or six inmates at most and to think that two of the five were me and Mike, two friends from the same neighborhood who went to the same prison at two completely different times, the odds of this happening are off the charts.

There are still two questions that I have with all of this and sadly, or maybe I should say, happily, Mike went home to be with the Lord..First what yard was Mike on, and second what pod and space was he in? If I ever find out that Mike was on the south yard in 2A7 I will collapse to the floor.

Mike helped in planting the seeds that would one day grow into a mighty harvest for the glory of God. Mike was in and out of jail for most of his life, Mike never married or had children. Mike never owned a home or a business. So to the world, Mike never amounted to much in life, but to God Mike was very successful. What Mike, my Brother in Christ lacked in worldly material wealth, he more than made up for in building up his heavenly riches for the glory of God. I loved Mike and I miss him, sadly Mike fell prey to the wolves of alcoholism, but I know deep in my heart that he loved the Lord with all his heart and just as he went before me to Kingman in helping to prepare the way in advance of my arrival all those years ago, I have faith that Mike has once again gone before me to prepare the way for my arrival in heaven someday.

This is the eulogy I wrote for Mike and I wanted to add it to this book for without the spiritual seeds of faith that Mike helped to plant all those years ago I would not be sitting here writing this book today.

MY BROTHER IN CHRIST MIKE McCULLOUGH,

I had written a eulogy for our good friend and brother Mike M. I was saving it for when we all got together again someday. I thought I would share it on FB but for some reason I couldn't seem to find it. I thought I had stored it on a USB, it's here somewhere so in the meantime I wanted to share with all of you a little bit of Mike's story. As you all know Mike had gone to prison a few years back, a few years have now become more like 15 years ago. When Mike got home he talked about his experiences in serving Christ in prison, but I never asked which prison he was sent to. Then, I went to prison in 2008. When I got to my final destination Kingman State Prison in Kingman Az, the Body of Christ was on fire for the Lord, the Church of Kingman Prison had an army of Pastors and volunteers coming in to teach Bible Studies and a few other programs like Maximized Man, Celebrate Recovery, AA Meetings, the Speakers Forum just to name a few. The way that the Church was structured at the time was with a Head Chaplain and an Assistant Chaplain, 3 inmate Chaplain's Clerks which were paid positions, probably at 25 cents an hour or so.. Then we had what's called a Pod Pastor in each pod, then 3 Head Pastors who oversaw the Pod Pastors for each of the 3 yards...

I became a Pod Pastor and I was elected by the Body of Christ through the leadings of the Holy Spirit to be the Lead Pastor of the South Yard, which is one of the greatest honors of my life. (YES South Side of the sky) There is a lot more to this story but I want to keep the focus on Mike. I came home in 2010, by that time Mike was involved with the Salvation Army. By the time we hooked up again we had become Brothers in Christ, then a few years later I asked Mike what prison did he go to, He said Kingman and that he was hired has that prison's first Chaplain's Clerk, I just about fell off of my chair.

I began telling Mike about the Church of Kingman and about all the programs and about the praise and worship band and about the Pod Pastors and Head Pastors of each yard and that I had held those positions in the Church. He then informs me that he and the other 2 Chaplain's Clerks and Chaplain Eddie sat and prayed and talked about and started all the things that I was involved with. Mike our friend and brother was part of planning and growing the Church that I would one day serve in.

Mike told me that Chaplain Eddie anointed all the pods and cells of that prison and claimed that place has being Holy Ground for the glory of God, The Idea that two friends from the same neighborhood would one day have such an incredible impact on Kingman Prison and on the lives of hundreds even thousands of inmates is a testament to the awesome power and glory of God...

Then right before Mike died I asked him who facilitated the Inmate Bible Study while he was there? HOLD ON TO YOUR SEATS, he told me he did and I looked at him with shock and amazement and said, "So did I" The inmate Bible Study was very special because it was inmates only and it was just us and the Lord... You have to understand very few people in the history of that Prison were given the privilege of leading that Bible Study, probably between the time that Mike was there and the time that I was there were less than six inmates who facilitated that Bible Study and to think that me and Mike were 2 of them blows my mind. Many members of the Body of Christ at Kingman wanted to lead that Bible Study the person leading was handpicked by the Head Chaplain to lead it...

The Apostle Paul teaches us that one person plants and another waters and God provides the increase. We see this truth all to clear with me and Mike, Mike helped to plant the seeds of faith, I came at a later time unknowing to each other and helped in watering those seeds and God provided the increase for His glory... Mike's life was not a waste, not by a long shot, what he helped to start through his faith in Christ Yeshua has produced a mighty harvest that continues to grow to this day...

I miss my Brother in Christ Mike, I love him and I know he has once again gone before me to help prepare the way... I pray that during this Christmas Season that whoever reads this and has not yet invited Christ to come into their lives in genuine repentance, and love will please do so, so that we can all be together with Mike and our loved ones someday, standing in God's Glory and basking in the love of Christ Yeshua in Heaven...Amen John 14:27 John 3:16

1 Corinthians 3:5-9 Who then is Paul and who is Apollos but ministers through whom you believed as the Lord gave to each one? I planted Apollos watered but God gave the increase. So then neither he who plants is anything nor he who waters but God Who gives the increase. Now he who plants and he who waters are one and each one will receive his own reward according to his own labor. For we are God's fellow workers: you are God's field, you are God's building...

My Blessings

CHAPLAIN PAUL D. VESCIO

The Prayer of Salvation

Abba Father, I need a Savior. I cannot go on living like this any longer. I confess that I have sinned and I am truly sorry for not living my life in a way that is pleasing to You. I am in desperate need of a Savior God. I confess of my sins and I invite Your Son Christ Yeshua to come into my life. I thank You O Lord for Your forgiveness, mercy, and love. I surrender my life completely to You Lord in genuine repentance and love, and from this day forth I will do my very best in living my life in a way that's pleasing unto You, I love You and praise You... In Christ Yeshua's Holy Name I pray...Amen

John 3:16 For God so loved the world that He gave His only begotten Son that whoever believes in Him should not perish but have everlasting life...

Romans 10:9-10 That if you confess with your mouth the Lord Yeshua and believe in your heart that Abba Father raised Him from the dead you shall be saved. For with the heart one believes unto righteousness, and with the mouth confession is made unto salvation... Amen

Update, on October 25 2019, my 57 birthday, I called Kingman State Prison and found out that Mike was housed on the south yard possibly in the same building that I was.
(South side of the sky by Yes)

33 Christian Seeds for the Soul

Christian Seeds for the Soul is a compilation of 33 inspirational Christian poems and writings. These are only some of the many poems and writings that I have written over the past ten years, all for the glory of God. Some of these poems and writings were written while I was an Inmate at Kingman State Prison in Kingman Arizona.

My website is miraclesofkingman.com

A Prayer Of Five Scriptures
by Chaplain Paul D. Vescio 6-2010

O Lord You are my Shepherd, You bring me to a place of peace and rest by the still waters of tranquility. For You are the vine and I am the branches. I abide in You in peace and in love. You guide me continually, You satisfy my soul in drought and strengthen my bones. I am a well watered garden because of Your Spirit and love.

For You have prepared a place for me and You will come again to receive me to Yourself, You are the Way the Truth and the Life, for Your Word says,"Come to Me all you who labor and are heavy laden and I will give you rest," for I rest in You O Lord…

I will take Your yoke upon my life and learn from You, for You Lord are lowly in heart; gentle and yet all powerful. I find a place of peace and rest in You, for Your yoke is easy and Your burden is light.

You O Lord are my lighthouse by the sea that leads me out of all of life's storms and sets me safely into the light of Your love for now and all eternity in Christ Yeshua's name I pray…Amen.

John 14:27 Peace be with you…

A Cross To Bear 4-9-11

One faithful day our Father in heaven reached down to earth to plant the seed of a very special tree,

And with the passing of time, sunshine and rain the little tree began to grow in the midst of so much sorrow and pain.

Then the tree and the Son began to grow as one, the Son with wisdom and strength, so too the tree with strength and majesty,

you see the Father planted this special tree on His only begotten Son's very first birthday.

The tree provided shade and rest for the Son, it's branches became home for nesting birds and shelter for the animal's young.

Father and Son spent many hours sitting under their tree, for they knew it's true purpose in healing all humanity.

And then in the Son's 33rd year our Father in heaven looked down and shed a tear.

For with a lightening bolt and a violent storm, the mighty tree fell back to the earth from which it was born.

Now this was not something bad from the sky up above, you see this was done because of our Father's infinite love.

Then men came and proclaimed what they had found, they brought back some of Pilate's soldiers and cut the tree down.

The soldiers of iron cut the tree and hauled it away, they made it into crosses to be saved for yet another day.

On Good Friday the tree and the Son now hung as one, the true purpose of their existence on earth had now only just begun...

John 3:16

ABBA FATHER'S LOVE 9-7-2019

There's a patient in the care center where I serve as a Community Chaplain who does not believe that God loves her. We will call her Virginia. Virginia also believes that she is being punished by God because of all of her health care conditions and because of all of the hardships that her family is going through. I visit with Virginia often and I told her that we would go on this journey in search of God's love together. I set about by first asking Abba Father in prayer to please help me in finding some real answers to Virginia's questions. Abba Father directed me to John 3:16 as an example of His divine and everlasting love. I set about in asking Pastors and family members and friends this question,

What do you say to someone who doesn't believe that God loves them?

In time I would come to realize that it's not so much in what we say that matters as in what we do that truly matters in showing the love of Christ to all those around us.

One of many Scripture verses that the Spirit of God led me to while on this journey was Hebrews 6:10 in The Complete Jewish Study Bible.

For God is not so unfair as to forget your work and the love you showed for Him in your past service to His people and in your present service too.

Abba Father shows His love through His Son Christ Yeshua and Christ Yeshua shows His undying love through all those who place their faith, hope and love in Him. Christ Yeshua lives in all those who have accepted Him into their lives. Christ Yeshua pours His love into us, His true followers, His love is then poured out on to others by us through faith.

Yes Virginia there is a living God Who loves you very much, for He will never leave you nor forsake you. His love is with out end and even though you may be in pain and filled with great sadness and sorrow always remember weeping may endure for a night but joy comes in the morning. Christ Yeshua gave of Himself willingly out of love for all of us. He took our place and paid our sin debt in full by dying on the cross so that we as believers could be saved and spend eternity with Him in heaven.. Amen

And Let There Be Light 8-23-2010

In the beginning God created the heavens and the earth, the earth was without form and void, and darkness was on the face of the deep. And the Spirit of God was hovering over the face of the waters. Then God said, "Let There Be Light." (Genesis 1:1-3)

And there was light...

When life has changed from here to there and your heart is filled with the sadness of despair, reach out your hands to Christ Jesus and Let There Be Light for He is always there.

And if your heart becomes broken as though no one seems to really care, speak to Christ Yeshua in a soft, gentle whisper of a prayer, and Let There Be Light for He is always there..

And when the weight of this world is more than you or I could even bear give all of your burdens to Christ Yeshua,

and Let There Be Light for He is always there...

And when at night you find yourself sad and blue not knowing quite what to do, always remember our Lord Jesus loves each and everyone of you. For He always knows exactly just what to do, He will wipe away every single tear and chase away all of the darkness and all of your fear.

For our Lord's love fills us with peace, love and a hope as He places us into His care,

And Now Let There Be Light for He is Always There...Amen.

My Blessings

Coconuts 11-23-09

Now growing on a tiny island very far away are the coconut palms that began to sway.

A breeze blew in from the sea with love, as the Lord was watching from the sky above.

Down below a man was sleeping with simple ease, as a coconut fell off in the tropical breeze, it fell and hit him right in his head,

I tell you man for a moment I thought he was dead.

Then he jumped right up and praised God with such joy, "I thank you O Lord for this poor boy, for I was thirsty and hungry and look what fell my way, a coconut when the palms began to sway. And even though I had a bump on my head I praised God for what I was fed."

So the next time things look dark, rainy, and gray, take the time to find your blessing for a more bright and sunshiny new day,

In Name of Christ Jesus we pray...Amen

Crown and the Cross 7-31-2019

What the world can't grasp and what true believers in Christ Yeshua now know is that when we give our lives to Christ we receive both a crown and a cross. To the world the cross is all about loss and a crown of thorns is no crown for a king at all. Listen to the words of the The Apostle Paul who reminds us that to the world the riches of Yah are foolishness and worth nothing at all, then Paul continues to say that he equates material wealth as being rubbish with no real value at all, this compared to the eternal riches of God and His infinite power, glory and love. You go Saint Paul!!!

As believers in Christ Yeshua, The Crown and the Cross are symbols of our salvation, and of Christ Yeshua's victory and pain, Son shine and reign, and of His power, compassion, forgiveness and infinite love. The Crown and the Cross are also a great source of inspiration and hope, in fact it's through Christ Yeshua's suffering and pain that we draw great inner strength and it's through His victory at Calvary and having been raised from the tomb, that the Body of Christ shouts,

HALLELUYAH!!! HALLELUYAH!!!
HALLELUYAH!!!

PRAISE YAH FOR HIS BRIDE AND GROOM
AMEN!!!

As believers in Christ Yeshua we have been given both a crown and a cross for the glory of Abba Father, for the word of God says,

Philippians 3:8

Yet indeed I also count all things loss for the excellence of the knowledge of Christ Yeshua my Lord for Whom I have suffered the loss of all things and count them as rubbish that I may gain Christ. (Read verse 9)

1 Corinthians 2:13-16

These things we also speak not in words which man's wisdom teaches but which the Holy Spirit teaches comparing spiritual things with spiritual.

But the natural man does not receive the things of the Spirit of God for they are foolishness to him nor can he know them because they are spiritually discerned. But he who is spiritual judges all things yet he himself is rightly judged by no one. For who has known the mind of the Lord that he may instruct Him? But we have the mind of Christ.

1 Corinthians 3:18-20

Let no one deceive himself. If anyone among you seems to be wise in this age let him become a fool that he may become wise. For the wisdom of this word is foolishness with God. For it is written "He catches the wise in their own craftiness." and again "The Lord knows the thoughts of the wise that they are futile."

1 Peter 2:9-10 The Crown

But you are a chosen generation a royal priesthood a holy nation, His own special people that you may proclaim the praises of Him who called you out of darkness and into His marvelous light, who once were not a people but are now the people of YAH who had not obtained mercy but now have obtained mercy...

Matthew 16:24-26 The Cross

Then Yeshua said to His disciples, "If anyone desires to come after Me let him deny himself and take up his cross and follow Me. For whoever desires to save his life will lose it but whoever loses their life for My sake will find it. For what profit is it to a man if he gains the whole world and loses his own soul or what will a man give in exchange for his soul?"

John 3:16   Matthew 11:28-30   Luke 9:23-26

Feed My Sheep Nov. 5 2018

There's an empty chair sitting by my bed, O Lord I cry out just wanting to be fed. There are nurses and staff running all around, but the word of God is no where to be found, for I am stuck in this prison of a bed only wanting to be fed. O there once was a time when I was spiritually fed, there once was a time when I sprang right out of my bed. I would rise early in the morn, I would dine on the Lord's word feeling newly reborn.   Then being filled with the Spirit of God I kicked the devil right in the head having now been satisfied by our Lord's Holy Bread. I put on the full Armor of God, fully ready to begin the battle of the day, but first I bowed my head and I started to pray,

"Abba Father I love You, Holy Spirit I love You, Christ Yeshua I love You, This is the day that the Lord has made we will rejoice and be glad in it because we walk by faith and not by sight, Now faith comes by hearing and hearing by the Word of YAH (God) Holy Spirit take charge over our lives, guide us, shape us and mold us into the likeness of Christ Yeshua, lift us up in the positive, wash out the negative and help us to serve Yeshua in humility and love, Please bless this day and our loved ones in the Name of Christ Yeshua we pray...Amen There is a hope a hope that can not be denied, there is a peace a peace that cannot be denied, there is forgiveness,

forgiveness that cannot be denied and there is a love a love that cannot be denied, His Name is Christ Yeshua our Lord and Savior...in His Holy Name may we all be healed and Spiritually fed through His love and forgiveness and by His Holy Bread...Amen John 14:27

My Blessing

Imagine 5-5-2019

Imagine looking off to the east and watching as a beautiful sunrise peeks over distant snow capped mountains. Imagine you're sitting with Christ Yeshua in a beautiful garden filled with an endless number of colorful flowers, now imagine being filled with great peace, joy, comfort and love as the two of you spend time together. You see this isn't just any garden this is your heavenly garden of Christ that Abba Father has provided just for you. This very special garden is your heavenly garden that stretches without end.

Imagine seeing all of the brilliant colors of the rainbow in what seems to be an endless variety of colorful flowers that leaves you completely awe struck .

Now Imagine looking up overhead and seeing as seven vibrant colorful rainbows seem to fill the sky above. Imagine that there are endless rows of lush green apple trees all around you, all of which are filled with delicious red apples the size of baseballs.

Imagine that Christ Yeshua invites you to walk with Him through your heavenly garden, and as you both begin your faith walk together our Lord begins to talk about His life and about the promise we have of an everlasting life in Heaven with Him. His words are sweet as honeycomb and they bring great comfort and peace to our aching souls.

Your walk with Christ leads you to a peaceful stream of running water that's teaming with life and just ahead you can see a small waterfall that leads into a pond of fresh clear blue water. Catfish, rainbow trout and bluegill are seen jumping in the air and splashing in the water as the morning mist rises off of the calm blue waters. Imagine sitting with Our Lord by the still waters of peace and tranquility as ten thousand colorful butterflies take to the air.

Imagine as blue birds, red robins and white doves fly too and fro. Imagine as the lion and the lamb are seen resting peacefully together near by.

Imagine as our Lord Christ Yeshua anoints your head with oil and fills your cup so it over flows and as He reassures you of your salvation and of your place in heaven. He tells you that He loves you with all His heart and that He will never leave you nor forsake you, He encourages you with His Word.

The Seven I Am Statements of Christ Yeshua

John 6:35-48, I Am The Bread Of Life, He who comes to Me shall never hunger and he who believes in Me shall never thirst...

John 8:12, I Am The Light Of The World. He who follows Me shall not walk in darkness but have the light of life...

John 10:7-10, I Am The Sheep Gate (The Door) "Yes indeed I tell you, I Am the gate for the sheep."

John 10:11-18, I Am The Good Shepherd. The Good Shepherd gives His life for the sheep.

John 15:1-5, I Am The True Vine, I Am the Vine and you are the branches, he who abides in Me and I in him bears much fruit for without Me you can do nothing.

John 14:6, I Am The Way, The Truth and The Life, no one comes to the Father except through Me.

John 11:25-27, I Am The Resurrection And The Life, he who believes in Me though he may die, he shall live...Amen

"You can do all things through Christ Yeshua Who strengthens you" ... Philippians 4:13

Inspire 2012

Tear drops are the gateway to the soul, For with eyes wide shut the light of our Lord Jesus pierces deep into the very depths of our hearts.

Eyes are no longer needed to see with, the eyes of our hearts have now been forever opened by the power of God.

We begin to see things in a whole new and glorious light.

We are now walking in the Spirit of God, we no longer need our sight, for we walk by faith and not by sight.

The warmth of God's saving grace and love cascades through my soul like the falling droplets of a gentle spring rain.

As I stand in awe of Your holy presence and love, I am healed, comforted and forgiven. I am forever grateful for the life that You gave so that I may live.

"My child I will never leave you nor forsake you. Pick up your cross daily and follow Me in obedience and in Love. For in so doing you my precious child will indeed inspire others.

Through your example hearts will be opened, darkness will be cast out and the light of Christ Jesus will shine on through...

"As you travel through the journey of life always remember to keep the eyes of your heart firmly focused on Me, and when things in this life get rough and overwhelming and you begin to worry and tire, just reach out to Me in faith and love and

"INSPIRE"

Psalms 23 The Lord is my Shepherd July 16- 2018

The Lord is my Shepherd I shall not want, (Abba Father supplies all of our needs, we are lacking in nothing.) He makes me to lie down in green pastures, (Abba Father leads us to a place of peace and rest.) He leads me beside the still waters. (Abba Father brings us to a place of refreshment and replenishment.)

He restores my soul and He leads me in the path of righteousness for His namesake. (We are saved through the shed blood of Christ Yeshua and we give all of the glory to YAH. Abba Father sets us on the right path. In Israel when a sheep keeps going astray the Shepherd will brake the lambs legs in order to teach it not to run away and risk being eaten by predators .

Abba Father sometimes does the same thing in our lives, if we continue to want to go astray all the time Abba Father in His infinite wisdom and love will break us in order to teach us to stay on the right path in life. He loves us that much that He would rather break our legs then to have us run off and be ravaged by the wolves of this world, we give all of the glory to Him for keeping us safe.)Yea though I walk through the valley of the shadow of death I will fear no evil for You are with me. Even though there are times in our lives where we walk in dark valleys You are there. After the Shepherd breaks the lamb's leg he carries the lamb on his shoulders until the lamb is able to walk on its own again and in doing so the lamb will never stray again. In the same way our Lord carries us when we are broken so we will never go astray from Him ever again...

Your rod and staff comfort me. (The rod and the staff are the same thing it is used as a tool in keeping the lambs together and it is used as a weapon in fighting off predators. (Knowing that when we walk in the valley of the shadow death and through very dark and very scary times in our lives He is always there with us, guiding, and comforting us and protecting us, for His word says that He will never leave us nor forsake us...)

You have prepared a table for me in the presence of my enemies, (Even though there are predators and forces of evil all around us Abba Father has provided a safe place for us to eat and rest and as believers in Christ Yeshua we each have a special seat with our names on it at the wedding feast of Christ...)

You anoint my head with oil, (Anoint my head with oil, found through Google. Author unknown.)

"Sheep can get their heads caught in briers and die trying to get untangled. There are horrid little flies that like to torment sheep by laying eggs in their nostrils which turn into worms and drive the sheep to beat their head against a rock, sometimes to death. Their ears and eyes are also susceptible to tormenting insects.

So the shepherd anoints their whole head with oil. Then there is peace. That oil forms a barrier of protection against the evil that tries to destroy the sheep.

Do you have times of mental torment? Do the worrisome thoughts invade your mind over and over? Do you beat your head against a wall trying to stop them? Have you ever asked God to anoint your head with oil? He has an endless supply! His oil protects and makes it possible for you to fix your heart, mind, and eyes on Him today and always!

There is peace in the valley! May our good good Father anoint your head with oil today so that your cup overflows with blessings! God is good and He is faithful!!"

My cup overflows, (The word of YAH fills our Spirit and is satisfying to our soul. When we read the word of YAH and Abba Father reveals His truth to us through the leadings of the Holy Spirit we overflow with excitement and can't help but to want to run out and share it with all those around us.) Surely goodness and mercy will follow all the days of my life and I will dwell in the house of the Lord forever and ever...Amen

Abba Father's goodness and His mercy will be blessed upon me all the days of my life and I will dwell with Him in Heaven for ever and ever...Amen John 14:27

My Blessing

The Gardener 10-15-2012

Blessed are you who with a little faith, hope and love sow the precious seeds of life into the fertile soil of our hearts.

Blessed are you who with your kind words of understanding, compassion and love make ready the soil of our hearts for planting.

Blessed are you who along with the Living Water of life water the seeds so they can grow.

Blessed are you who take the time to help us to remove the thorn bushes and weeds that have grown totally out of control in our life, choking our faith and blinding our eyes.

Blessed are you who with the passing of time help to nurture our garden and help us to grow.

Blessed are You who prune our branches and ready us to bear fruit for the glory of Elohim

Blessed are you who help harvest our fruit and then share it with those who are hungry so that they can one day grow a beautiful garden of their own.

Blessed are you gardeners of Christ Yeshua, in reaching out to the lost souls of this world by helping others to grow a true garden of Eden of their very own for the glory of Elohim in Christ Yeshua's name...Amen

Psalms 65:9-13

You visit the earth and water it,
You greatly enrich it;
The river of God is full of water,
You provide their grain,
For so You have prepared it.
You water it's ridges abundantly,
You settle its furrows;
You make it soft with showers;
You bless its growth.

You crown the year with Your goodness,
And Your paths drip with abundance.
They drop on the pastures of the wilderness,
And the little hills rejoice on every side.
The pastures are clothed with flocks;
The valleys also are covered in grain;
They shout for joy they also sing...

Our Daily Bread 10-8-10

There's a hunger that lies deep within our weary souls that only the spiritual Bread of life can satisfy.

For it sustains us through the peeks and valleys of our life. This is God's special gift from heaven that He shares with us in the dawning of each new day...

And when we find ourselves struggling through a spiritual wilderness, our Daily Bread is always there to help nourish and strengthen us. Now this is not a bread of pumpernickel, wheat, barely, or rye, this Bread is the Son of God that He sent for you and I...

The Bread of life is our Lord and Savior Jesus Christ, for they are One in the same, and with the dawning of each new day we as a body partake in the manna of life as we read the Word of God and pray to Him in peace and love each day...Amen

(John 1:1-3 plus 14) In the beginning was the Word, and the Word was with God, and the Word was God, He was the beginning with God. All things were made through Him and without Him nothing was made that was made, and the Word became flesh and dwelt among us, and we beheld His glory, the glory as of the only begotten of the Father, full of grace and truth...Amen

(John 6:35) And Jesus said to them, "I am the bread of life.

He who comes to Me shall never hunger, and he who believes in Me shall never thirst"...Amen

My Blessings

The Bridge

by Pastor Paul D Vescio 4-5-11 rewrite Chaplain
Paul Nov.11 2018

Cold steel, a blank stare, crashing waves, darkness closing in all around me even though the dawn peeks over the horizon. People rushing by beneath my feet, do they know, do they care and even if they did could they even stop me if they tried? And by the way how can a man with no shoes cross this raging sea? Is this what my life has come to be, a desperate man standing on the edge of time suspended in space ready to jump into the unknown depths of silence for all eternity? I now find myself standing one step away from finding out the truth, is there a reason for all that there is? Eden, hell, or nothingness is now within a single footstep,

"O God please send me a Savior."

Then in the sudden stillness of time I watched as a pair of doves glide gently by. A deep breath, a memory and then a soft whisper of a dream begins to call my name, "PLEASE DON'T JUMP!!!" Come down please, I'm here to help you, please come down from up there!!!"

"Why should I?"

"BECAUSE GOD IS STILL SETTING THE STAGE!!!"

Are you feeling overwhelmed in life? Do you feel as though you're standing out in the rain waiting in a long line that feels like it's never going to move forward? The reason why we find ourselves waiting on God is because He's still setting the stage for the next big act in our lives. He's putting together the cast of people, He's building the sets and He is making ready the path that we soon will be standing upon. Think of it this way, a group of people are traveling on a bus through the hot southwestern desert, suddenly steam begins shooting out of the radiator, soon you find yourselves stuck on the side of the road in the middle of July with no one in sight.

As you all begin to pray to God for His guidance, help and blessing you all look in utter amazement as a stray horse is seen walking in the distance. You all realize that if you can catch him then one person could ride ahead for help. Your able to catch the horse then you place your full faith in the rider who then rides off to retrieve help and life giving water. You're calm and at peace having placed your faith and trust in him because you know deep in your heart that he will return to you. Why are you so sure? Because the rider is your father and the group of people that you are with is your family. It is the same way when we find ourselves caught up in a dry desert of problems reaching out to God and having faith that He will provide His latter rain in our lives so as to quench our thirst.

We have faith that our Father in heaven has instructed His Son Christ Yeshua to go ahead and prepare a place for us. Christ Yeshua provides us with His living waters of life, for He is constantly setting the stage for the next exciting new season in our lives...Amen John 3:16 John 14:27

John 14:1-4

Let not your heart be troubled you believe in YAH believe also in Me.

In My Father's house there are many mansions if it were not so I would have told you. I go to prepare a place for you. And if I go to prepare a place for you I will come again and receive you to Myself, that where I am there you may be also, and where I go you know and the way you know...Amen

The Candle Light of God 1-12-11

Faith, Soft gentle snowflakes created in a perfect image now take to flight, lifted into the air by the breath of God...

They dance through life on the many memories that they themselves have so gracefully made. And with the passing of each new day they draw a little closer to the Light that calls their name.

The painted sands that once upon a time fell ever so slowly now seem to fall increasingly faster with each new day. And then one day upon an awakening in time we realize that our time here on this earth is but a fleeting moment.

The sands continue to fall right before our weary eyes, our outer self is fading away, the pain with in this outer shell that we call a body is held in check by the inner peace, and love of Christ Jesus...

Day turns to night, night gives way to day, the Dr. visits, the tests, the hurt, the pain, the chemo, a time to reflect, a time to cry, and yet even in the midst of the storm we find the time to laugh, to hope, and to share some joy, it's a time to forgive, a time to draw closer to Jesus and a time to say "I love you."

Sands continue to fall and yet with each passing grain we draw closer to the Light, the Light surrounds us, comforts us and fills us with an inner peace and love. The Light warms our hearts and heals or aching souls...

It is the sunset of our life, Hospice is now a place that we call home. Sands almost gone now, and with what little strength we have we reach out to the Light, the Light catches us and wraps us in His loving arms, and with our last breath here on earth we touch the Lord's heart and become the light of Christ for all eternity, in Christ Yeshua's Holy Name we pray...Amen

Like falling snowflakes that gently touch the light of God, as we leave this world and enter into the next we melt into the light and love of

Christ Yeshua for all eternity...Amen

John 3:16   John 14:27

The Chaplain 5-24-11

Can a man look deep with in a mirror and begin to see far beyond his own reflection?

Can he reach out in love to touch the hearts of all those who suffer while feeling their pain?

Can he himself become a prisoner in chains while visiting all those who are they themselves housed in prison?

Can he walk the lonely halls of a hospital and know that Christ is there walking with him?

Can he kneel by the bedside of someone who is in Hospice and yet pray as if that person was his own mother or father?

Can he visit sick children in a children's hospital late at night and yet still treat every child as if they were his very own?

Can he serve long hours without receiving a pay check because he knows deep in his heart the joy that he receives from God is something money can't buy.

Can a man or a woman reach out to hold the hand of someone who is sick and suffering then look into their eyes only to see the eyes of Christ looking back at them?

Can a person sacrifice their favorite T.V. Show like American Idol and then go out and serve Christ Jesus for the sacrifice that He gave for you?

There is just such a person in life and that person is your Chaplain...

My Blessing

The Eyes of Christ 3-11-11

What would you do if given the chance to look deep into the eyes of Christ?

Be still your mind and think about it for a moment then let the eyes of your heart be opened to see deep into our Lord and Savior's eyes.

For if we did dare to set sail together to dream of distant shores,what do you think we would find once we arrived?

And as we broke through the mist of the fog we could see on the beach that lay before us a small camp fire with one person sitting by its side. The man called out to us and invited us to join Him... Now about twenty five feet out I jumped into the water to pull the boat a shore. The man greeted us with open arms and shared some of His bread with the fish that he had cooked, and as we sat by His side He asked us this one profound question,

"You seek to look into the eyes of Christ? And what is it that you think you would see if given the chance?"

Maybe as we looked deep into the eyes of Christ we would enter into a place of peace and rest filled with milk and honey, a place where we could walk safely in green pastures and then sit beside the still waters of tranquility.

Or we might see an entire universe in the twinkling of His eye. We would see the Lion and the Lamb laying side by side together under the Tree of Life, and from the sky above a beautiful rainbow touches The True Vine then springs forth as the Bread of life is cast upon the waters of humanity...

Then He said,

"If you truly seek to look into the eyes of Christ then look no further than to gaze into My very own for they are His."

And as we looked into the Lord's eyes, Jesus revealed Himself to us... We began to see the faces of the homeless, the lost, the sick and the dying, in nursing homes, Hospice centers, mental institutions, the prostitute, the widows, the disabled and the poor, children in hospitals, in poverty, in wars, we saw the drug addict, the imprisoned, the infirmed, the battered wives, we saw the pain and the tears in our Lords eyes, then He said,

"As you look deep into My eyes and see all those who suffer, go and look upon them with the same love and compassion that I have for you and as you do you will see Me looking back at you, for we are brought together in oneness through suffering.

Now if you truly wish to look into the eyes of Christ look no further than into the eyes of all those who suffer... In Jesus name, Amen...

I see the Christ

When Mother Teresa was interviewed about her work with the dying and destitute in the streets of Calcutta, she said,

"When I look into their eyes I see the Christ"

Instead of passing her comment off as a noble shrug of modesty think about it, consider the possibility that she's telling the actual truth. Imagine how spiritually uplifted she must be all day long if she's looking into the eyes of Christ. Has she stumbled onto a secret about human service that most of us haven't yet awakened to?

Of course we can't get to that same point by imitating Mother Teresa's life. We have to begin guessing our own way, with as wide – open a heart and mind as possible. The point here is that service is an exciting lifestyle which we've been trained to ignore in favor of competition, profit, motive, recreation, and status, none of which have a very good track record of bringing lasting happiness.

Many times in our lives we're unsure of what to do next.

Maybe we've just gotten out of prison or are recently divorced, fired, unhappy or confused. Instead of making a feeble gesture of change – swapping one situation for another almost exactly like it, we have the opportunity to sit down and decide on what form of suffering touches us most, and go out and help fix it. Real change, real faith, real love...

Bees gather nectar, trees grow, garbage trucks collect garbage and servants serve others. No big deal; no credit due; just everything doing what's best for itself; everything following its own nature.

(This story about Mother Teresa is from a book that was given to me while I was in Kingman prison. The book is called, We're All Doing Time - a guide for getting free. by Bo Lozoff)

Matthew 25: 42-46 for I was hungry and you gave me no food;

I was thirsty and you gave Me no drink ;

I was a stranger and you did not take Me in, naked and you did not clothe Me, sick and in prison and you did not visit Me.

Then they will answer Him saying, Lord when did we see You hungry or thirsty or a stranger, or naked, or sick, or in prison and did not minister to You?

Then He will answer them saying, Assuredly I say to you, inasmuch as you did not do it to one of the least of these, you did not do it to Me... Amen (Please read verse 46)

My Blessing

God's Gift of JOY 12-9-12

Standing in the rain filled with so much sorrow and pain, why do the dark clouds of despair continue to haunt me day after day?

I saw a homeless man, he praised God then he tried to lift up my day, O why am I so sad as I sit in my BMW and drive away?

Now even as I drive and try to get away the dark clouds of despair continue to follow me throughout the day.

Turning the corner entering the on ramp that leads to the parkway that points the way home, I looked to see what appears to be makeshift houses made out of cardboard and still others crafted out of tin and Styrofoam.

Now traffic slows to a snail's pace, red and blue lights flash all around, I can hear the sirens of an ambulance as a hurt man lies motionless laying on the ground.

An hour later I finally pull in the driveway of my five bedroom home, and as I take a look I could see my poor neighbor standing outside in the rain talking on his cell phone once again.

I guess I hadn't really noticed but the rain had turned into snow and all of the Christmas lights were beginning to glow.

I sat in my car, boxes and bags of presents piled all around, my family in the house decorating and laughing but still I felt depressed and so dreadfully down.

"Hey Phil hows it going? Are you getting along Ok during this time of the year?" You see my neighbor Phil lost his wife Sara about six months ago and this was his first Christmas alone without her.

"We are all praying for you Phil, Merry Christmas."

Then I paused and had a thought, "Hey Phil, please come on over tonight for dinner and spend Christmas-Eve with us."

For with that one little act of kindness God opened His hand and placed a little joy into mine, and as I stopped looking at my self and began to look towards the light of God's Son the clouds of despair seemed to just float gently away, for God had given me the gift of His Son's joy on this Christmas Eve day.

You see happiness comes from happenings, but Joy comes from above.

Psalms 30:5 Weeping may endure for a night,

But joy comes in the morning.

The Haves and the Have Nots 3-26-10

The have nots live in big houses,

The haves don't need a big house.

The have nots want the newest car,

The haves are content to walk.

The have nots are always complaining,

The haves are always giving thanks.

The have nots love money,

The haves give it to those in need.

The have nots are never satisfied,

The haves are at peace.

The have nots hate their neighbors,

The haves love thy neighbor.

The have nots hold unforgiveness in their hearts,

The haves forgive all those who have hurt them.

The have nots are blind,

The haves spiritual eyes have now been opened...

The have nots want to own and rule the world,

The haves want nothing to do with the world.

The have nots think material wealth will bring
them happiness,

The haves know that only the love of Christ
can fill a person with forgiveness, peace, joy and
love...

So don't be a have not, filling your life with meaningless junk and material wealth.

Be a have by opening your heart to Christ Yeshua and inviting Him in so you can have a meaningful personal relationship with Him, in Christ Yeshua's Holy Name I Pray...Amen

Matthew 16:24-26 Then Yeshua said to His disciples,

"If anyone desires to come after me let him deny himself and take up his cross daily and follow Me.

For whoever desires to save his life will lose it, but whoever loses his life for My sake will find it.

For what profit is it to a man if he gains the whole world and yet loses his soul, or what will a man give in exchange for his soul?

John 14:27 And Christ Yeshua speaking to His Disciples said, "Peace I leave with you, My peace I give to you, not as the world gives do I give to you, let not your heart be troubled neither let them be afraid."

The Joshua Tree 2014

Burning sands shifting beneath my feet as the hot desert air transforms itself into a whirlwind of dust and sand; it's devilish hand seems to want to reach for my soul as it rises high up into the afternoon sky.

Birds of a feather are all to careful to avoid this whirling, swirling dust devil, for they too do not want to risk being caught up in its violent grasp.

And even in the midst of this blinding storm of dust, wind and sand you continue standing tall praising God as you lift up your hands, for in the safety and comfort of your cool shade we find the tortoise and the hare resting side by side, in fact all of God's creatures of this dry desert land come seeking refuge out of the blistering sun and the heat of the day.

Then finally a little mercy as the setting sun begins to melt away in the afternoon sky like a water color dream. The cool air brings a welcomed sigh of relief as it slowly chases away the heat of the day.

And still you stand firm praising God as you wait patently for the fulfillment of His promises and God's gift to the desert of His latter rain.

It's now nightfall and under the light of a full moon you stand always ready with a heightened sense of anticipation and hope as you look to the east and wait faithfully for our Lord's triumphant return.

The tortoise and the hare safely home for the night as the darkness brings forth the badger and the fox, rattlesnake,and coyote. And even as these predators seem to be nipping at your heals you continue to give God thanks and praise giving Him all the glory, because as you cast your bread upon the waters He is always faithful to lift your spirits on high.

O Joshua Tree you are yet another example of God's love and creativity in the midst of all of life's storms and adversity, for we give God all the thanks, praise, honor and glory as you continue to make a faithful stand.

You see we too are on a journey to fulfill God's master plan as we continue on our walk of faith with our Lord Christ Jesus through this hot, and dry hostel land...

Thank You Lord for all of Your blessings and for all of Your love in Jesus name I pray...Amen

Joshua 24:15

And if it seems evil to you to serve the Lord, choose for yourselves this day whom you will serve whether the gods which your fathers served that were on the other side of the river or the gods of the Amorites in whose land you dwell. But for me

and my house, we will serve the
Lord...Amen

Joshua 10:25

Then Joshua said to them, "Do not be afraid nor
be dismayed; be strong and of good courage, for
thus the Lord will do to all your enemies against
whom you fight."

My Blessings

The Lion And The Lamb 2-17-11

A single gull cries over head as gray skies seem to swallow up the sea. Crashing waves and turbulent winds grab at my very soul.

The hand of God pulls me close to the waters edge as the sands of time slip away beneath my feet.

I now begin to hear the cries of all the lost souls who find themselves drowning in the sea because of a lack of faith.

Fear comes over me as the sea calls out my name, and I, like so many before me must now walk it's length in-order to reach the promise land.

As I take my first steps onto the sea of death the water grabs at my heals and pulls me in up to my waist and neck, now as I shake and tremble with fear I cry out to God for help.

"O Lord, I believe in Your Son Jesus, for Your word says that You would never leave me nor forsake me. Please Father God send me Your Son to deliver me out of this sea of death in Jesus name I pray...Amen

Suddenly the water grabs at me and pulls me completely under, and in a state of total desperation I reached out to Jesus. Then as though in a far away dream I felt the grasp of a gentle hand begin to pull me back up and out of the water.

As I opened my eyes I found myself in the presence of an angel of the Lord, She was glowing and radiant in the spirit of God. She had soft golden hair, a flowing white silken gown, wings with feathers the finest in all creation. She looked at me and said,

"As you begin your journey across the sea keep your eyes on Jesus for He will not let you drown... "Believe"

Now standing on the water I found my self alone once again, I noticed the more fearful that I had become the more fierce the Storm became all around me.

Then out in the far off distance a tinny light appeared. The closer I walked towards the light the more at peace I became.

I knew in my heart that this was the light of Christ Jesus. And with each passing step of faith I took the calmer the wind and waves became.

I could now see three images walking towards me, Jesus was clearly in the middle and to His right a snow white lamb scared and pierced. And there to His left a lion powerful and magnificent and yet they seemed to know me and put me at ease.

The Lighthouse by the Sea
8-28-2013

Mourning light shimmers off of the clear blue sea as captains and crew set sail chasing after a dream.

And as they leave the rocky shore line behind, the lighthouse stands as a symbol of peace and of hope for all who would dare to try to challenge this unforgiving body of water.

It's now the afternoon and the catch is good so we stay until sunset with talk of riches and fame, glory and happiness, maybe a new car or if we could make a catch like this all summer, even a down payment for a new house. Swordfish, tuna, halibut and sea bass line the hulls of many a fishing vessel as they crisscross over what would seem to be a sea full of riches.

It is now night fall, a full moon hides behind a row of gray billowy dark clouds. The smell of rain is in the air, then a warning on the radio of an impending storm headed our way.

The Captain makes the call, "time to head home."
A rolling fog fills the air as the pouring rain begins to fall. Soon crashing waves would begin tossing the ship side to side with howling force winds, at times sounding like a runaway freight train. With visibility

so low the ship's only guides are now it's compass and the hand of God.

Crashing waves continue to pound the ship, then one of the ships engines burnout under the strain of so much stress. Captain's orders, all of ship's cargo is to be dumped in the sea or all will be lost. And still no sign of land. Two hours, then three, then four, still no relief, the ship is now taking on too much water, a distress signal goes out to all ports, "MAY DAY!!! MAY DAY!!! WE NEED AS-SISTANCE!!! MAY DAY"!!!!

THIS IS FISHING VESSEL 193, MAY DAY"!!!

Suddenly and without warning our other engine stalls. The ship is now at the mercy of the sea's crashing waves. Tossed and turned about like a cork the crew frantically tries to restart one of the en-gines. Then in the midst of the storm the Captain pauses and begins to pray to God for the safety of his ship and crew.

"Lord please help us to return safely home to our families. Please God help us to restart one of the engines, Lord please allow Your shining light to safely guide us back home. I thank You Lord, In Je-sus name I pray...Amen."

"Captain, Captain, I see a light off of the port side Sir. I think it's the Lighthouse Sir"

Just then the ships engine restarted, "Praise God" shouted the crew. The Captain began steering the ship toward the tiny white light that lie just ahead.

The Light seemed to call the ship in the right direction, moving with the ship pointing the way home. The captain thought it only seemed that way because of the storm and that our eyes were playing tricks on us.

And there, two lights could be seen. One a little closer out to sea the other clearly atop a mountain side.

As we struggled to make it back into port we noticed the Light that was closer seemed to merge with the light a top the mountain.

Soon a Coast Guard cutter would came along side and escort us safely back home. I asked the captain of the cutter, "What was that other Light we saw at sea Sir, was that this ship."

"No, he said, "we came out from Pershing Point, there were no other ships out in this area at that time."

(Fear is the opposite of faith, and faith means
to trust)

Lighthouse by the Sea Part 2

We are the captains of our lives sailing about in a sea of humanity, but in the light of day we have little or no need for the lighthouse by the sea.

The light of day represents the good times in our lives when things are going well for us. You know, plenty of money, a good job, a cool car and maybe even a family with a nice new home. Fun, Fun, Fun till Daddy takes the T-Bird away!!!

The dark storms we face in life are all of the trials and tribulations that we must endure. We can not even begin to appreciate the Light unless we've been made to walk through the darkness.

The crew in the story caught a big hall of fish in the light of day under clear blue skies. They didn't give thanks to God for His blessings. They had no need for His light in the light of day. (during the good times) They thought only of themselves and what they were going to do with all the money that they thought they were going to make. They didn't give all the glory to God or even ask Him through prayer how they should share the money in serving His Son Christ Jesus.

When the storm blew in the crew of the ship realized that the only thing that truly mattered in life was life itself. Suddenly money, fame, and glory, the catch of the day, a new car or the possibility of being able to buy a new house didn't mean anything to them any more. What truly mattered then was God and His saving grace. They now had a new found appreciation for the Light, for it was the Light that was now leading them out of the darkness and safely back home, whether they made it back home here on earth to be with their families or made it home to heaven to be with God, they were saved.

"Sometimes we must endure the darkness of life's storms in-order to truly appreciate the light of Christ's life... Amen"

John 8:12

And Jesus spoke to them again saying,

"I Am the light of the world. He who follows Me shall not walk in darkness but have the light of life"...Amen

Peter Sees The Light Matthew 14:22-33

Immediately Jesus made His disciples get into the boat and go before Him to the other side, while He sent the multitudes away.

And when He had sent the multitudes away, He went up on the mountain by Himself to pray. Now when evening came He was alone there.

But the boat was now in the middle of the sea, tossed by the waves because the wind was contrary.

Now in the fourth watch of the night Jesus went to them walking on the sea.

And when the disciples saw Him walking on the sea they were troubled saying, "It is a ghost!"And they cried out for fear. But immediately Jesus spoke to them saying, "Be of good cheer, it is I, do not be afraid."

And Peter answered Him and said, "Lord if it is You command me to come to You on the water."

So He said, "come." And when Peter had come down out of the boat he walked on the water to go to Jesus.

But when he saw that the wind was boisterous, he was afraid; and beginning to sink he cried out saying,

"Lord save me!"

And immediately Jesus stretched out His hand and caught him and said, "O you you of little faith why do you doubt?"

And when they got into the boat the wind ceased. Then those who were in the boat came and worshiped Him saying, "Truly You are the Son of God."

When Peter kept his eyes firmly focused on Christ he walked on water without any fear. But when he took his eyes off of Jesus and focused on the waves and the raging storm he became fearful and sank in the water. Peter magnified his problem which was the storm and minimized Christ Who is our Savior.

When we focus on God and His Son Jesus we minimize our problems, Oh the storm is still there but the fear is lessened when we put our faith and trust in Christ Jesus. When we maximize God we minimize our problems, when we maximize our problems we minimize God and His saving grace through His Son Jesus' love...Amen

My Blessings

The Little Christmas Tree
11-24-09

Way down deep in the misty green forest of the mighty Christmas trees, there lived the tiny little village of the Look-at-meeeezzzzzz.

Now all of the Look-at-meeeezzzzzz were only out to please; themselves that is with simple ease. They always tried to out do the other, I tell you man it was always brother against brother.

Yes it was always brother against brother, you see they didn't take the time to care very much about each other.

Then one Christmas-Eve they all got a really bright idea, "Hey let's see who'll give the Pastor the biggest Christmas gift this year.

Well I tell you that was it, they all ran over each other, pushing, yelling and shoving on one another, I tell you man it was brother against brother as they all set out to out do each other.

They ran straight down to the stores and they cleaned them all out, then they pushed their way into the church without even a doubt.

And there they all were piling junk upon junk trying to out do the other, I tell you it was a mad house, brother against brother.

They were all pushing and yelling, it was quit something to see, then one of the Look-at-meeeezzzzz shouted out,

"Hey Look At Me"!!!!!!!!!

"I have the biggest Christmas gift, wait, just wait you'll see."

Now while all this mess was going on, a little girl walked in form the church back door, you see she had only a little Christmas tree to give because she was so very poor.

And in the midst of all the pushing and yelling she softly and gently set the little Christmas tree down upon the stone church floor, then she tip toed back out the old church door.

Then the Pastor came in and said with a smile, "Oh now that's the nicest Christmas gift that I've seen in a while. You see friends Christmas isn't about stuff or things or about how much you have, or about tarring each other apart, it's about the love of Christ Yeshua through your very own heart, and It's about love, forgiveness, family and joy, you see it's about helping one another in the true spirit of love as we celebrate the birth of God's little Boy...

Then after all of the Look-at-meeeezzzzs had heard what their Pastor had said they all fell to their knees and bowed their little heads.

And has they all prayed upon their knees, they stopped thinking about themselves and only as they pleased.

Our Lord had opened up their hearts and allowed them all to see, Praise God for they're now called,

"Hey Look-it's-Not-About-Meeeeezzzzzzz"

Yes they all thanked our Lord for opening their eyes to see, as they all sang a song of thanksgiving around the little Christmas tree.

And on that faithful lit night, the light of our Lord Christ Yeshua did shine so heavenly bright.

Then they all held hands by candle light as they all sang a song of peace, and love called Silent Night. And now all of the,

"Hey-it's-Not-About-Meeeezzzzzzs"

would very much like to wish all of you a very Merry Christmas and a very blessed night, in the name of Christ Yeshua may you all be blessed and may you all be healed by His heavenly light...Amen

The Angles Announce Jesus to the Shepherds

Luke Chapter 2:8-14

Now there were in the same country shepherds living out in the fields, keeping watch over their flock by night. And behold an angel of the Lord stood before them and they were greatly afraid.

Then the angel said to them, "Do not be afraid, for behold I bring you good tidings of great joy which will be to all people.

"For there is born to you this day in the city of David a Savior who is Christ the Lord.

And this will be a sign to you; You will find a Babe wrapped in swaddling cloths lying in a manger."

And suddenly there was with the angel a multitude of the heavenly host praising God saying;

"Glory to God in the highest, and on earth peace, goodwill toward men." Amen

John 3:16

For God so loved the world that He gave His only begotten Son, that whoever believes in Him should not perish but have everlasting life...Amen

The Son Will Come Out Tomorrow 10-25-09

And through the darkness of the night, we have the promise of Christ's light. And though life's storms may blow our way, our Lord is faithful to always up lift our day.

And even though you're in so much pain and sorrow, cheer up for the Son will come out tomorrow. Fear not for the word of God says, He will never leave you nor forsake you...Amen.

He is the light of our life without any doubt so proclaim the good news as you lift up your voice and shout.

For He will wash away all of your tears and all of your sorrows as you walk with Him in love knowing that,

The Sun will come out tomorrow...

Yes the Son will come out tomorrow, for the night is far spent and the day is at hand, the victory has already been won, as you now stand in your victory garden in peace and love with

God's only begotten Son.

And now always remember, no matter how dark the night or how deep the sorrow, Father God is always faithful in love with the promise, His Son will always come out tomorrow...Amen.

"Peace I leave with you, My peace I give to you, not as the world gives do I give to you, let not your heart be troubled, nether let it be afraid"...Amen. John 14:27

Revelation 7:17 for the Lamb who is in the midst of the throne will shepherd them and lead them to living fountains of waters and God will wipe away every tear from their eyes...Amen

My Blessings

The Train 7-4-09

"O Great horse of iron and steel, spewing smoke and breathing fire, eating wood and coal, drinking water, releasing steam high into the air, rolling free down your tracks. Locomotive of light-ening, thunder and steal, your cars that you pull like so many little children holding hands all in a row. Passengers delight in all of your power and speed.

The Conductor calls out,

"Tickets Please"

Now some tickets lead us on a path of right-eousness and still others on a one way ticket straight into hell.

As we continue to travel down the narrow track light turns into dusk, then into darkness of the night, caboose passes by laughing and singing and is gone in the blink of an eye.

Then entering a tunnel, dark and void of the light our train comes to a sudden stop, some of the passengers are let off right into outer darkness; why?

Starting once again on our way, passing through time and space I begin to question, "where, when, how and why?"

Moving ever faster now, time seems to stand still and bend, a long dark night gives way to the sweet morning light.

Coming into the station it's the dawning of a brand new and glorious day. As the train comes to a rolling stop we are told to leave all of our belongings behind, we won't be needing them anymore. Stepping off of the train I can now see why, For standing before me is a Kingdom of light shining so Heavenly bright, love, song, gates of pearly white, a million angels stand at attention singing as ten thousand doves take to flight.

People cheer and sing, laugh and shout. All the Saints help the new arrivals off the train.

Then the engineer steps out and into our sight, with hands and feet scared, a crown of thorns, a flowing white robe and snow white hair He says,

"Welcome home my good and faithful children; "I love you"

And so my faithful friends always remember when the train of life comes at the end of life make sure you have the ticket of Salvation and Righteousness for it will surely save your life,

in Christ Yeshua's Holy name I pray...Amen
(John 14:27)

John 3:16 is truly our Golden Ticket of Life.

The Water's Edge 3-7-11

Alone in my thoughts, I stood at the water's edge and watched with sudden anticipation as a single black raven hovered just over head.

The waves rolled gently in as the setting sun melted quietly into the sea. A sudden gust of wind and the autumn leaves of yesterday began to dance and swirl all around me.

And yet still, there it was, the same daunting question that has been haunting me for an entire life time,

"Is there more to this life then what we live here on earth? "

I began to walk along the shore line once more, feeling cold and alone I looked out to see as a beautiful sunset gave way to dark gray skies. A sudden chill caused me to pause and pull my coat tightly around my neck. I could hear the cry of a lone seagull off in the distance, hunger set in, but the search for an answer to my question kept me walking in the opposite direction of home.

The rhythmic sound of the waves now made me stop once again and wonder, a wave travels across the sea then at the end of its journey the wave crashes onto the shore line and ceases to be, is that how our simple lives here on earth are?

Do we travel through life on a sea of time only to one day hit the shores of death and cease to be?

I began walking and as I pondered this question with a sense of despair I noticed something, the incoming waves hit the shore line that much was true but then they embark on a brand new journey back out to sea.

I realized with a new found sense of hope that what we humans deem as the end of life is really just the beginning of a new and glorious journey back home to heaven with God...

As I turned around and began my journey homeward filled with hope a voice called out to me and said,

"Have faith my child, cast your bread upon the waters and let Me heal your soul"

On the surface I didn't understand what the Lord was trying to tell me, but deep in my heart I slowly began to understand and in an act of faith I cast my bread upon the waters. Then I realized that the end of life is actually a new beginning for the word of God says in John 3:16

For God so loved the world that He gave His only begotten Son that whoever believes in Him should not perish but have ever lasting life...

Peter 5:6-7 Therefore humble yourselves under the mighty hand of God that He may exalt you in due time casting all your care upon Him for He cares for you...

A life without faith in Jesus has no hope and is meaningless, Christ gives us a future and a hope through His sacrifice, word and His love for all who put their faith and trust in Him...

The life which we now live is but a stepping stone through time as we walk on a sea of love with Christ Jesus and on into heaven for all eternity...Amen

My Blessings

The Yellow Brick Road

by Pastor Paul D. Vescio 12- 4- 09

There's a road in our lives that sets the pace for right and for wrong, it's filled with all kinds dreams disappointments, ups and downs, the road of life is filled with magical wonder a colorful sounds.

Around the next bend apple trees dance in the wind and then the scarecrow becomes your best friend.

You travel a little bit further down the yellow brick road and what do you see, the Tin Man standing perfectly still by the old oak tree. And as he stands not making a sound, you anoint his head with oil, with the oil can you had found.

Then finally being able to move and to speak, he looks at you and says, "You know I feel as though I'm falling apart, you see I have this empty awful feeling way down deep in my heart."

"Well then come along with us, we wont let you fall apart, you see we're going to the Emerald City they'll fix up your empty heart.

And with that all three were back on their way in the hopes of making it to the Emerald City that day.

Now you enter into a place that's a little dark and very scary, then with a thump and a great roar, the sound of which scares you to the core.

Then out from the trees, A ROAR!!! A LION,
    "O HELP US PLEASE!!!"

The lion jumped right out looking for a fight,
and then with a gentle slap to his face he's filled
with a terrible fright. Then you wipe away his tears
and find out he's lost and afraid and not very brave,
so you help him up and say. "Now come along with
us we'll get you saved."

And with that you all continue down the yellow
brick road in search of something wonderfully told.

O but along life's way came an evil witch,
she was out to achieve satan's evil wish. She offered
Scarecrow a fiery dish saying, "Hey Scarecrow what
do you think, go a head and make a wish." She
tempted them with all kinds of goodies, sins, and
lies, but in the end they cast her away and ran for
their lives.

Finally in the distance there shined an
illuminating light, it was the Emerald City shining
so beautifully bright.

Now running with all of their might, they all ran
towards the heavenly light.

Soon they arrived at the gates of the city of
light, and with a quick knock on the door said,

"Please Sir we're all spiritually poor."

And with that a voice answered from up above,
"Just open your hearts and be filled with My love."
Right then the love of Christ Yeshua came in like a

flood for we had all been reborn of the Spirit, Water and of the Blood.

Yes they had all been saved through the Spirit, Water and of the Blood and that my friends is the Good News, for Christ Yeshua had saved them from a life time of sadness and singing the blues.

So on this faithful day always remember what's been told, and be sure to walk down the road of life with Christ Yeshua, down life's Yellow Brick Road...

In the Name of Christ Yeshua name pray...Amen.

Tracks of Grace May-20-11

Can a man get hit by a train and live? Well I would have to say no, no that is until last week when just such a thing happened. You see I had just arrived at the Dream Center for Wens. night service and as I was walking in the lobby three brother's in Christ were running out the door, they said that a man had just been hit by a train across the street. I turned and went back out side and to my surprise no one ran across the street to his aid. The next thing I knew I was running across the street.

A man and a woman were already there, they had called 911 for help, I could hear the sirens of the fire and police. I walked over to the man and told him my name and asked if I could pray for him, he sat still, not complaining or crying out in pain and said, "Yes" I began to pray and as I did I could not help but to have compassion for this man for here was a man who bore the scars of someone who had been crucified. He had cuts, scrapes, bruises, and the markings of someone who had been whipped, he was bleeding; drops of blood dripped to the ground as I prayed with him.

I could see the Christ in all of this, and the more I thought about the man and how he looked and acted the more of Christ Jesus I began to see.

I wanted to write a story or a poem about the man who was hit by a train and lived. But a report with a parable would be more effective.

My Blessing

The Parable of The Tracks of Grace

An Angel of the Lord took me up on a high mountain peak and asked, "What do you see?"

I answered and said,

"I see train tracks as far as the eye can see."

"Now look a little closer and tell me what you see."

I answered and said,

"I see people, many millions of people tied to the tracks."

"Who are they." I asked.

"They are the lost and unsaved, for they are those who have yet to be born again but only if they themselves so choose. They have become bound and tied spiritually to satan's train tracks of death because of their choices in life. This has happened because they themselves have chosen to believe the lies of satan and reject the love and the truth of Jesus Christ...Amen

You see their sinful nature and selfish pride in the absence of a personal relationship with Christ Yeshua has left them set under a yoke of bondage, they have become imprisoned by the powers of darkness because of their own disbelief.

"Is there nothing that we can do to help them?" I asked.

"You can help them but first you must know their pain"

Then suddenly and without warning a violent wind lifted me up into the air, I was now in a turbulent whirlwind being tossed and turned about like a lost kite and when it finally stopped I found myself tied and bound to the very same tracks that I was supposed to go and help free others from.

I couldn't move an inch but I could still speak. I tried desperately to free myself but nothing of my own works could release the cords that bound me. Then as I looked down the tracks I watched in horror as the earth split open and give way to hell it self.

I could hear the blowing of a chilling whistle as a thunderous ROAR shook the earth all around me. Then the darkness of hell gave birth to a violent black locomotive driven by satan himself.

He was coming with all his fury to take my life, I had now only a few short minuets to do something. Than in the midst of the horror and pain I began to pray,

"O Lord please help save me, for I put all of my faith and trust in You...Amen"

And there the train of death came spewing steam and smoke, with sparks flying and now so close that I could see the face of satan laughing at me. I closed my eyes and then a voice said,

"My child I have come to take your place on the tracks."

Jesus reached down and released the cords that had me bound, He set me free and out of harms way, then as He took my place and laid down on the tracks that lay before me, He told me to go and help lead others to Him so that they could be set free too.

He said that He loves me this much that He would lay down His life for me. And as He looked into my eyes and spoke these words of life into my soul satan's train hit with all of it's fury...

I sat there stunned, I was filled with both gratitude and great sadness.

Jesus had saved my life by sacrificing His own. I cried as I sat with my hands to my face thanking Him in prayer.

Then the Lord Christ Yeshua walked over to me in a glowing white robe and put His hand on my shoulder, I thanked Him as I cried and wept at His feet.

For it was only then that I fully understood the true depths of HIS love for me, for He took my place and died so that I could live.

John 3:16-17

For God so loved the world that He gave His only begotten Son that whoever believes in Him should not parish but have everlasting life.

For God did not send His Son into the world to condemn the world, but that the world through Him might be saved.

My Blessing

Victory Through Adversity Written
by Chaplain Paul 2017

Shipwrecked on a deserted desert island a solitary man tries to cope with the sadness and pain of loneliness...

Where there once were the comforts of a family and a home, he now finds himself half starved and homeless.

Each day he prays for deliverance from his tiny island prison. Little by little with each passing day he presses on as he builds a small little hut for himself out of palm leaves, sticks, grass and mud. He keeps his prized possessions of handmade tools, weapons, bowls, food etc. stored there. All that he has after 2 years of being marooned is kept in his little island hut.

Then one day while climbing up a mountain slope to see if there were any ships in the area he suddenly noticed black smoke billowing up to the sky. He watches in horror as his little island hut goes up in flames. By the time he ran back down the hill in the hopes of saving what little he had it was to late.

Now as he sits in the sand crying, having lost everything he looks to the sky and screams,

"God how could you have let this happen to me, I lost everything I had, WHY GOD WHY!!!"

One day later a ship came to shore and rescued the man, when asked, "How did you know I was here?" The rescue party answered, "We saw the smoke from your signal fire." God can turn what appears to be our greatest defeats in life into our greatest victories for His glory... Amen

Proverbs 3:5-6, Romans 8:28, John 14:27,

Isaiah 41:10

My Blessings

The Raven and the Dove 8-7-2015

The Raven takes to the air by night, his soul void of kindness and the love of Yeshua's heavenly light. His heart full of anger, want, and greed, he will stop at nothing to take and watch you bleed.

The Dove, bird of peace, hope, forgiveness and love, he will lift your spirits and fill your hearts with Christ's unwavering love, he is the light of our Savior, the messenger of peace, for he bears witness to Abba Father's grace, mercy, forgiveness, and love...

Today we watch and see the raven and the dove circling high above, the dove bearing witness to Christ Yeshua's compassion and love, The raven striking at the dove, for the raven despises anything to do with the Elohim's peace and infinite love...

The dove fights back with prayer, forgiveness, understanding compassion and love, the raven circles around, heart struck, beaten, then falls suddenly to the ground, now broken, scarred and in pain, he begins to feel the sting of Christ Yeshua's heavenly reign.

Repent O raven, repent, broken, shattered, beaten, scared and now all alone, the raven gives his life completely to the only true Savior known...

Morning light, the Son's warmth heals the raven's tortured soul making him spiritually right; now with the righteous wings of snow white he takes to the sky in the midst of Elohim's heavenly light, The raven now transformed into a righteous dove because of Christ Yeshua's infinite love.... Amen

2 Corinthians 5:17 A new creation in Christ

My Blessings

Living Waters

Water colors of an afternoon sunset seem to want to melt gently off the page like a distant rainbow of light that touches the water,s edge.

Colorful tropical birds of a hidden rain forest sing in perfect harmony just over head, they seek a cool pool of living water so as to replenish and bask in its healing presence and beauty.

A caravan of thirsty camels slowly walk across the shifting sands of a distant painted desert. In the distance awaits an oasis of living water, a family of elephants take time to rest a midst the swaying palm trees of this unforgiving land.

A crying new born is comforted by his mother's love, she begins feeding him of the living waters of life that she had so quietly stored away.

The clear blue waters of the sea are the living waters of life that a school of dolphins live and play in. The coral reef is home to millions of colorful sea creatures, for them these pristine clear blue waters are a true breath of life.

These living waters of the sea are seemingly without end. But there remains still one source of living, life giving waters that are without end. For these living waters of life are the waters of salvation that one receives through their faith and love in Christ Jesus...Amen

For Jesus speaking to the Samaritan woman by the well said, "If anyone drinks of this water they will thirst again, but if anyone drinks of the water that I shall give, they will never thirst again, for the water that I shall give will become in them a fountain of living water springing up unto everlasting life"...Amen John 4:13-14

The Living Waters of Salvation
bring forth new life to our spiritually
dead dry bones...

Ezekiel Chapter 37:1-14

Latter Rain 10-23-2016

Still water, a blanket of fallen ash, a fiery hand snatches away what little moister remains in the air, the earth cracks as the dry grass fades away. Pillars of brown smoke reach high up into the afternoon sky.

Night fall brings forth a candle lit forest as the tops of pine trees light up a moon lit sky; in the midst of which all of God's creatures run for their lives.

Hand sown seeds placed carefully within fertile soil, a crop of green soon bursts forth into the sun's light. Soon after the heat of summer holds back the rain. Fields of green quickly dry up and wither away as hope begins to fade under a hot summer's sun.. Days now turn into weeks with no rain in sight, and then we paused and prayed for rain...

A broken heart, a hug goodbye, a ship leaves port and heads out to sea. A battle fought, a battle won but still the anguish and the pain of waiting.

And then one day, expectation, anticipation, jubilation with thanks and praise as God fulfills the promise of His latter rain in our lives and suddenly we're renewed once more in the glory and blessings of God, in Christ Yeshua's Holy Name I pray...Amen.

The Anointing Oil of Latter Rain
Use of this fragrance might offer hope,
encouragement and incentive to someone needing
to stand firm as he or she eagerly awaits the
fulfillment of all of the promises of God...

(source Mary's Lavish Gift by Wm I. Bill Edmunds)

The Latter Rain Part Two

Foot steps through the hands of time leads the faithful onward to the promised land of God as parting waves give birth to autumn fields of grain.

Snow capt mountains like a reflection of light in an eagle's eye seem to touch the rising sun and then suddenly begins to melt away.

Two are now on a journey of One, the hand of God cradles us in His loving arms as we cradle His Son in ours. Our walk of faith is but a new beginning that will one day bring forth God's latter rain of salvation for the world...

Then in an instant, traveling through a measure of time, a Savior is baptized and a season of renewed hope and faith has finally begun.

And now walking by faith with the chosen twelve our Lord gives the gift of sight to the blind so they can begin to see the world through His eyes.

For He brings healing to the sick and the maimed so they can sing and dance, He raised the dead and even helped over five thousand hungry people to be spiritually fed.

But even in the midst of sharing our Lord's daily bread He told us of His sacrifice and eminent dread. He even said that there was one among us who would betray Him, whom satan had lied to and falsely led.

And even with something as simple as a kiss, the safety and warmth of the light of day suddenly became the cold terrifying darkness by night, then we became scattered with fear and with pain, as we all prayed for the mercy and love of God's latter rain.

Nails of iron now pierce through bone and skin upon an old splintered cross, our Lord's precious blood was all but poured out and lost.

And then by sun down He gave of His last breath, He was then taken off of the cross and laid to a powerful rest, then we all cried and mourned together because of our Lord's terrible death.

On Sunday we all gathered together as one, then in the midst of our sorrow and pain, a knock on the door revealed our Lord Christ Yeshua for He had risen again.

Our Lord and Savior Christ Yeshua appeared to us with His gift of salvation, hope and love, healing our sorrows and all of our pain, for a loving Father had wrapped the gift of His Son's salvation and love in His Latter Rain... John 3:16-17

God's gift of grace through faith is but a latter rain upon a spiritually dry and hopeless land.

For the latter rain of Christ Yeshua is a welcome sigh of relief to those who hunger for the bread of life and thirst for waters of salvation with forgiveness, understanding, peace, hope and love, in Christ Yeshua's Name I pray...Amen

Psalms 65:9-13

You visit the earth and water it,
You greatly enrich it;
The river of God is full of water;
You provide their grain.
For so You have prepared it.
You water its ridges abundantly,
You settle its furrows;
You make it soft with showers,
You bless its growth.
You crown the year with Your goodness,
And Your paths drip with abundance.
They drop on the pastures of the wilderness,
And the little hills rejoice on every side.
The pastures are clothed with flocks;
The valleys also are covered with grain;
They shout for joy they also sing.

Our Victory Garden

Given to me by Brother Israel in Kingman

To find your Place of worship look into your pain and find your praise, every low place in your life prepares you for your high place, and every tear you cry is water for your victory, and even though your in the valley, victory comes through your adversity to find your place of worship...Amen

As we stand in our victory garden with Christ Yeshua God is faithful to water it with all of the tears of sadness that we cried in life. For tears of sadness, sorrow and pain are now forever transformed into tears of great joy by the grace of God's transcendent glory and love, in Yeshua's Name...Amen

Psalms 56:8 You number my wanderings;

Put my tears into Your bottle;

Are they not in Your book?

When I cry out to You;

Then my enemies will turn back;

This I know because God is for me.

In God (I will praise His word)

In the Lord (I will praise His word)

In God I have put my trust;

I will not be afraid.

What can man do to me?

May our Lord bless you and fill you with His peace and love in Christ Yeshua's Holy Name I pray...Amen John 14:27

To Pastor Paul,

The Book which started out to record miracles has turned into so much more as I read through the book I realized that what we deem as a miracle God considers His daily work. Our God is in the business of miracles and He never ceases from His work.

Possibly the greatest miracle here in recorded made in this book is made in the one who carried this book. Yes Paul you are that great miracle. You were once sick and dying and God made you well. You were on a road to eternal separation from your creator and God changed your direction. You were once doomed to hell and now you have citizenship in Heaven.

You were once a criminal now you share the love of Christ. All who come in contact with you are blessed you have changed many lives because of your miracle which God gave to you.

Paul I charge you to always keep this book of miracles and always remember from where you came. Chaplain Wayne and Sandy

Written in the Miracle Book of Kingman State Prison

There were so many miracles occurring at Kingman while I was there that we decided to document them in a book called The Miracle Book. Chaplain Basye gave me the book so that I could go forth and proclaim the Miracles of Kingman...Without a doubt, the greatest miracle of all was in the countless number of inmates who gave their lives to Christ while serving time at Kingman State Prison.

Thank You Abba Father for all of Your Blessings, Guidance and Love in helping me to become the Community Chaplain of God that I am today, and Thank You Abba Father for helping me to write this book, I give all the Praise, Glory and Honor to You in Christ Yeshu'a Holy Name...Amen

John 14:27

Seeds of a Dandelion

by Chaplain Paul Vescio Oct. 27 2019

The Holy Spirit touches our souls like droplets of pure rain water.

Then we take to the air as the Spirit of God lifts us on high. The Holy Spirit carries us gently through green pastures and leads us to the still waters. We touchdown upon fertile soil as we give Abba Father all the glory. Soon we begin to grow and bear fruit for the glory of God. The fruit we bear is a reflection of Christ's love. The Son's love warms our hearts and gives us great peace and comfort. Our cup runs over as we can't help but to share Christ's love with others.

We now see with the eyes of our heart as we walk by faith and not by sight. For Your word is a lamp to our feet and a light to our soul. We know O Lord that You will never leave us nor forsake us as we place our faith, hope and trust in You. We are the seeds of Christ's light as the Holy Spirit carries us across deserts and oceans, mountains and plains. We carry the truth of God's word and the hope of an everlasting life through Christ the Lord...Amen

Psalms 36:7-9 How precious is Your loving-kindness O God!

Therefore the children of men put their trust under the shadow of Your wings. They are abundantly satisfied with the fullness of Your house. And You give them drink from the river of Your pleasures. For with You is a fountain of life; In Your light we see light...Amen

My Blessings

Books By Chaplain Paul D Vescio

Chaplain America John 316

Chaplain America John 316 Part Two by Feb. 1 2022

Fomba The Elephant Children's Story Book Series Books 1- 7

Christian Seeds For The Soul Books 1-2

Victory Over Suffering Through Christ Our Lord

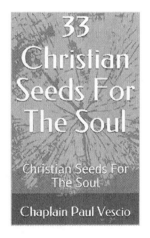

Philippians 4:13

I can do all things through Christ who strengthens me...

www.miraclesofkingman.com